With this book Wilma Derksen has found a way to redeem the seemingly irredeemable. After living through a parent's worst nightmare, she devoted herself to the hard work of forgiveness, dissecting each stage with a surgeon's skill. The practical wisdom that has emerged could only come from someone who strained to forgive the unforgivable—and somehow succeeded. What she learned along the way brings hope to all of us who struggle with this most difficult, yet most necessary task.

PHILIP YANCEY, editor-at-large, *Christianity Today*

I have followed Wilma's journey for years. It has been incredibly difficult, incredibly moving, and her insights incredibly profound. She has much to teach us all.

HOWARD ZEHR, Distinguished Professor of Restorative Justice, codirector, Zehr Institute for Restorative Justice, Eastern Mennonite University

In *The Way of Letting Go* Wilma Derksen demonstrates how the healing process is to pass from the narrative of trauma as overwhelming grief into the narrative of trauma as an experience of deep and meaningful significance. Bringing together all her experience and learning following the agony of her daughter's murder, here over thirty years later Derksen is able to give voice to a humanity born out of suffering. There are few who have given as much thought to

the transformative power of forgiveness—she has defined, refined, probed, and reevaluated one of the most difficult, complex, but never more relevant forces in the world today.

MARINA CANTACUZINO, founder,
The Forgiveness Project

Wilma Derksen's powerful book highlights a profound paradox—to achieve some degree of control over one's life and emotions in the face of grief and trauma, one has to do the opposite—let go of control.

TED WACHTEL, editor, BuildingANewReality.com

The answer is love and compassion for all of humanity. When the Nazarene said that we should forgive seventy times seven, he was telling us that forgiveness should be a habit, a way of life. Forgiveness is not for the person who has wronged us; it is for us—it sets us free. Wilma's story is proof of this.

BILL PELKE, author, *Journey of*
Hope ... from Violence to Healing

THE WAY OF LETTING GO

One Woman's Walk toward Forgiveness

WILMA DERKSEN

ZONDERVAN

The Way of Letting Go
Copyright © 2017 by Wilma Derksen

Requests for information should be addressed to:
Zondervan, *3900 Sparks Dr. SE, Grand Rapids, Michigan 49546*

ISBN 978-0-310-34657-9 (softcover)

ISBN 978-0-310-34824-5 (ebook)

Cover design: Curt Diepenhorst
Cover illustration: James W. Hall IV
Interior design: Denise Froehlich

First printing January 2017 / Printed in the United States of America

For my father …

Forgiveness is not an occasional act; it is a constant attitude.

—Martin Luther King Jr.

CONTENTS

ACKNOWLEDGMENTS

In the same way that it takes a village to raise a child, it takes a village to help us forgive. I want to acknowledge all those along the way who have helped our family walk the journey.

I am still thankful for the immediate response to our cry for help the day that Candace disappeared, November 30, 1984. People we had never met just pitched in: walking the street, searching the neighborhood, plastering the city with posters, and praying. Our church community, Candace's school, and the search committee from Cliff's work built a supportive community around us that held us together with their ongoing support and prayers.

I am thankful for the city's generous sympathy when her body was found seven weeks later in a shed not far from our house, her hands and feet tied. She had been abandoned to die in the freezing temperatures of a Winnipeg winter. They attended the memorial service and sent cards, food, and prayers.

I am thankful for the members of the Winnipeg police force who helped us look for Candace, exhausting all the leads, and who were able to contain the crime scene with such vigilance that the evidence they collected could stand the test of time. I am thankful for those in the force who rekindled her cold-case file and brought fresh thinking, new eyes, and amazing dedication to it twenty-three years later, and uncovered the narrative that led to an arrest.

I am extremely grateful for the trial that took place twenty-six years after the fact. I am grateful for the work of everyone who took part in it: the judge, the Crown, the defense, and the witnesses who worked vigilantly to uncover the story for us so that we could finally know the truth of what happened. Even a justice process that remains unfinished is still better than no attempt at justice at all. We continue to appreciate those who won't let it die. Their fight for justice is admirable.

I am grateful to all those who listened to my story over the years, asked important questions, and offered their support and wisdom along the way. Each presentation I made was a tremendous opportunity for learning.

I am grateful to the pioneers in restorative justice who included me in their discussions as they explored what forgiveness means between victims and offenders of serious crime. Their devotion to creating peace and reconciliation was a constant encouragement to keep me working at my own agenda of forgiveness.

I am grateful to my close friends who stood beside me, always offering a listening ear, support, encouragement, patience, and wisdom. They were my coaches, psychologists, and counselors. Without them I could not have made it.

I am grateful for my contenders, those who challenged me all along the way. They made me stronger.

I am grateful to my incredible family. I admire my husband, who is blossoming into the artist he has always wanted to be. Even though most of his life was lived against the wind of innuendo and suspicion, he never tired. He continued to live his life faithfully in service to his family and others. It is satisfying to see him finally able to devote himself to his passion for sculpting and teaching art to his students.

I am grateful to my two remaining children. Odia is an artist like her father and has proven to be amazingly creative in all areas of her life. She could have succumbed to fear, but didn't. She is the most courageous woman I know. She will travel through any blizzard with a smile on her face.

She married a special man, Larry, a true minister to the needy. The two of them now have a miraculous little girl, Georgia Wynne. Georgia, who was under two pounds when she was born, is proving to be a very determined and delightful spirit.

Syras, our son, is wise beyond his years. He constantly astounds us and others with his principled and gentle life. As a psychologist, he continues to help those around him grow as he himself grows. He married a lovely woman, Natasha, who is also a creative person and devoted to mothering. Simeon, their son, is articulate beyond his years, and Anna, their daughter, is showing herself to be a very warm and relational person. These two are also miracles.

Our family dinner discussions are always invigorating, stimulating, encouraging, and so fun. Fun is important to me.

I am still grateful for Candace and the opportunity to love her—even after all these years.

I am grateful to all the people who had a vision for this book when I didn't have the confidence to even think of writing it. The encouragement to write this book was astounding.

I am especially grateful to my God who fashioned this Tree of Forgiveness for us—right outside the Garden of Eden—a tree that gives us the opportunity to transform everything negative that we experience into something life-giving.

—WD

Two roads diverged in a wood, and I—
I took the one less traveled by,
And that has made all the difference.

—*ROBERT FROST*

An Introduction by Malcolm Gladwell

Some years ago, I met a man named Mike Reynolds. I went to his home in Fresno, California, and sat in his study as he told me the story of what had happened to his eighteen-year-old daughter, Kimber, twenty years before. She had been out to dinner with a friend in downtown Fresno when she was set upon by two young men—both convicted felons. They shot her in the head. She died a day later.

On the wall behind Reynolds, there was a photograph of Kimber. In the kitchen next door, there was a painting of Kimber with angel's wings, ascending to heaven. "I literally held her hand while she was dying," Reynolds said. "It's a very helpless feeling." At that moment, he told me, he made a vow.

"Everything I've done ever since is about a promise I made to Kimber on her deathbed. I told her, 'I can't save your life. But I'm going to do everything in my power to try and prevent this from happening to anybody else.'"

What Reynolds did was start a public campaign to dramatically stiffen California's criminal penalties. It was called Three Strikes. Criminals convicted of their second offense would see their sentences doubled, and the measure called for those convicted of their third offense—regardless of how serious it was—to face a mandatory prison time of twenty-five years to life. Reynolds led a statewide referendum on Three Strikes. He won. Three Strikes passed into law in California, beginning a two-decade experiment in punitive justice without parallel in the modern, developed world. California spent billions of dollars on new prisons. On a per capita basis, California—by the turn of the century—had seven times as many people behind bars as Canada or Western Europe. People received life sentences for the most trivial crimes: in one case, for stealing a slice of pizza. When the measure was finally repealed in 2014, the consensus among criminologists was that the law had achieved almost none of its goals. It had locked up thousands of people at great social and financial cost with no discernable effect on California's crime rate.

Over the years, many people have come to Fresno to speak to Reynolds about Three Strikes and his daughter's death. It is Reynolds's habit to take his visitors to the Daily Planet—the restaurant where his daughter ate before she was killed across the street. I heard about one of those visits before I made the same journey. Reynolds had gotten into an argument with the restaurant's owner. She told him to stop bringing people around on tours. Reynolds was harming her business. "When will this be over?" she asked him. Reynolds was livid. "Sure, it's hurt her business," he said, "but it's wrecked our lives. I told her it will be over when my daughter comes back."

Reynolds wanted to take me to the Daily Planet as well. I said no. This was two and a half hours after I had first sat down for our interview, and the intensity of his emotion was too much for me. I could not find in him even the slightest hint of peace, forgiveness, or reconciliation with what had happened.

Reynolds reached across the table and placed his hand on my arm.

"Do you carry a wallet?" he asked. He handed me a passport-size photo of his daughter. "That was taken a month before Kimber was murdered. Maybe set that in there and think about that when you open your wallet. Sometimes you need to put a face with something like this." His daughter had been dead for twenty-five years. But to Reynolds it was as if it had just happened. "That kid had everything to live for. To have something like this happen, to have somebody kill her in cold blood like that ... It just has to be stopped."

That afternoon in Fresno broke my heart.

Not long after my visit to Fresno, I went to Winnipeg to see Wilma Derksen, whose book you now have in your hands. I heard about her story from my sister-in-law, who is—like Wilma—a Mennonite from Manitoba. I have to confess, looking back, that my reasons for making the trip were a bit jumbled. I was writing my book *David and Goliath* and was interested in people's responses to adversity. Mike Reynolds had taken one approach: to avenge his daughter's death. Wilma had lost her daughter under equally tragic circumstances and, I had learned, had taken a very different path.

The contrast between the two of them—between Fresno and Winnipeg—was striking. Writers are drawn to contrasts like this: they are our bread and butter. I would write about their stories side by side, I decided.

But in truth the narrative requirements of journalism played only the smallest role to go and see Wilma. I was *shaken* by my visit with Mike Reynolds in a way that I am rarely shaken by interviewing someone. Here was a man who had suffered an unimaginable loss and had managed, in his search for vengeance, to create even more sorrow and suffering with Three Strikes. Is that the way the world works? Does tragedy inevitably lead to greater tragedy? I found the thought devastating. Wilma's experience offered a ray of hope. So I flew to Winnipeg and sat with her in her backyard. And she told me a story that began almost exactly as Mike Reynolds's story began—with the worst thing that can ever befall a parent—only in her case with an entirely different ending.

I won't tell Wilma's story for her. In the pages that follow, she does it far better than I ever could. I will only say that she reminds us that there is another way out of tragedy. It is a long and hard and rocky path, but it ends in a place of peace and joy. I listened to one man's grief—and heard the temple crashing down around him. I listened to one woman's grief—and saw the light of God's grace. *The Way of Letting Go* is a beautiful and important book. It will open your heart.

MALCOLM GLADWELL

Chapter 1

THE ENDING AND THE BEGINNING

This year I vow to learn how to garden. I will be the Farmer of Love and grow in understanding and forgiveness.

—JAROD KINTZ

Memories are the key to the past, but not to the future.

—CORRIE TEN BOOM

At the end of the most horrific day, January 17, 1985, there was a knock on the door. I glanced at the clock; it was ten o'clock.

I opened the door, and there was stranger in black standing there against the dark night.

"I too am a parent of a murdered child," he said, introducing himself. My heart sank—I could feel the blood drain from my face. *Parent of a murdered child?*

I was now a parent of a murdered child. My identity was at stake. Around noon that day, we had just heard that the body of Candace, our thirteen-year-old daughter, had been discovered by an employee of Alsip Brick, Tile and Lumber Company as he was checking an abandoned shed on the yard.

Who was this man at our door? Every stranger was now a suspect. Everyone was a potential murderer.

"I've come to tell you what to expect next," he said.

It was hard to believe that only seven weeks ago we had been an unknown, unnoticed, happy family. Cliff, my husband, was working as a program director for one of the largest camps in the province, and we had three children: Candace was our oldest, Odia was nine, and Syras was three. I was working my way into a journalism career.

Candace had called me from school to ask me for a ride home. Ordinarily I would have, but time had slipped by me, and I was running late. I had asked her if she wouldn't mind walking home this time so that by the time she got home I would be finished with my writing project, and the planned festivities for the weekend could begin. I promised to buy party food for her sleepover that weekend.

She said she didn't mind at all and then told me, rather breathlessly, that she had just had her face washed with snow by "David." The way she said his name, I knew how special he was.

When she didn't come through the door at the expected time, a little after four, I had a sinking feeling. I quickly packed up the children and drove down the street looking for her. Then I went to pick up Cliff from the office. Once home, we started calling all of her friends and our friends and family until we exhausted our leads. Around ten o'clock we called the police. By this time we were in a state of panic.

Our daughter's disappearance sparked Winnipeg's most comprehensive missing person's search to date. Together with the cooperation of the city, we left no stone unturned in our search for her, plastering the city with posters reading "Have you seen Candace?" For seven weeks we pleaded with the public to help us find her, exposing our shattered lives to the whole city.

Now that her body was found, we knew for certain that someone had indeed deliberately abducted her that Friday, taken her to a shed, tied her hands and feet, and then left her there to die in the plunging temperatures of the winter's first extreme cold front.

She had been murdered. The search was over.

We were exhausted; it had been a full day already. After finding out from the police that her body had been found, we immediately drove to the hospital morgue to identify her body.

After that, everyone started to descend on our house. Our friends who heard it on the news came with food and words of comfort. Our house was chaotic.

Now this stranger was appearing at our door with the promise of answers that we were just beginning to ask ourselves.

"Would you like to join us?" I asked.

Together with the couple who was staying the night with us, we sat down at the kitchen table for a warm piece of cherry pie. I couldn't eat, but our guests needed something.

He immediately began to tell his story.

"My daughter was murdered too," he began.

That's when we recognized him from the TV news reports over the last few years. It was a well-known local story.

There were no tears as he talked—none. But then again, I could talk about my daughter without tears as well. It was odd. Sometimes I cried uncontrollably; other times I was emotionless.

I remembered the day a group of friends came to pray for us. I hadn't been able to cry with them—or pray with them. There seemed to be two categories: one for talking about the death of our daughter, when we would cry, and one for talking about the murder and the abduction, when we had no tears.

"She was murdered at the donut shop," he continued. I had the feeling that he had told his story many times.

As he spoke, I kept wondering what had compelled him to come to our house so late at night. What compulsion was this? His mind seemed to be stuck.

Then he admitted it. He said he couldn't work anymore because he couldn't focus on anything but the murder of his daughter. He told us every little detail of the day she was killed.

He went on to say that the murder had damaged his health. And his face was blotched with red; he looked like he was smoldering with an inner rage.

He pulled out his collection of black notebooks from his suit jacket. They were much like the ones reporters used back then. He had recorded all the court proceedings in those books, meticulously and in detail. There had been two court trials already.

He ranted against the justice system, going into greater detail than any of us cared to hear, but he was so obsessed with it all.

Then he started describing the perpetrator, the man charged with first-degree murder. He was absolutely confident that the man was guilty, describing him as evil. He knew every detail of this offender's public and private life.

"I will never rest … till there is justice." He said it in many ways over and over as if he were locked in a battle for his life.

He was as angry with the media as he was with the justice administration and the killer.

He kept shaking his head, "I've lost so much—everything."

He hinted that the relationships in his family were strained because he couldn't concentrate on anything else but the murder.

And then he paused. "I've even lost the memory of my daughter."

In other words, the act of murder had taken the life of his daughter, but the aftermath of murder had taken *his life*.

The worst part was that there was no end in sight for him. Approximately a month before, an appeal was upheld, and so another trial was called. He didn't know how he would be able to go through it all again. He said he just wanted it to be over.

We sat stunned and horrified. I couldn't believe what

I was hearing. I couldn't believe the audacity of his visit—coming to tell us all of this on the worst day of our lives. Yet I was fascinated by him and listened intently, sensing that there had to be a reason for his coming. Whether we wanted to or not, we needed to hear this.

Besides, I was identifying with parts of his story. We had already encountered some of his trauma ourselves in the last seven weeks as we had desperately searched for our daughter. I was quickly becoming familiar with the terror, the anger, and the feeling that our hearts were breaking—except that this break wasn't only emotional, it was also real pain. I had never experienced such intense emotional pain.

We had also been offered medication. I had declined, believing that if I had gone through the pain of childbirth with Candace without medication, I needed to resist it now as well. I needed my wits about me even more now—even though she was gone physically, the memory of her still needed my mother's attention.

I also knew the potential of what this trauma could have on our marriage and relationships. After Candace's disappearance, I hadn't allowed Cliff to touch me. Because I thought someone had abducted Candace to sexually violate her, the thought of intimacy was revolting. I had resisted for six weeks. It had left us both isolated, uncomforted, and stressed.

I knew the potential of the damage of the publicity that we had so deliberately and desperately cultivated but that would now remain focused on us. There had already been public misunderstandings of our ways of coping—and some disruptive family discussions because of it.

I was already obsessed with watching the neighbors. I suspected everyone of having something to do with her disappearance. My world had become suddenly very hostile. I felt I was sinking into my own personal abyss.

I couldn't read, eat, or breathe without pain. Sleep was elusive.

I knew exactly what this strange man was talking about.

At midnight, he noticed the clock on the wall and stood up quite abruptly. He looked exhausted. As a hostess, I wanted to say something to comfort him. But too exhausted ourselves, we did not have the energy or the skill to comfort him at that moment. I felt incredible sadness as he stepped into the dark, cold winter night alone and despondent.

After he left, my husband and I went upstairs to our bedroom and just looked at each other desperately. We were scared. We had just lost our child. Were we going to lose everything? Was this the beginning of a spiral of losses that would leave us like the man: dark, desperate, hopeless, and insensitive to everything around us?

There had to be another way.

Cliff and I just looked at each other in disbelief, numb. We knew we would not be able to sleep. We had just identified Candace's body. Every time we shut our eyes we could see her lying there so very still on the gurney. Minus her vibrant, sanguine personality, she looked so tiny, so vulnerable, her face etched with pain.

Chapter 2

THE ONLY QUESTION

> *Life is grace. Sleep is forgiveness. The night*
> *absolves. Darkness wipes the slate clean, not*
> *spotless to be sure, but clean enough for another*
> *day's chalking.*
>
> —FREDERICK BUECHNER

Lights from the TV cameras had dimmed, and I thought the press conference was over. We had spent the entire time talking about our daughter—relieved that we had found her, shocked that she had been murdered, and thankful for everyone who had been searching for her.

Just as we were about to leave, someone asked the question.

"And what about the person who murdered your daughter?"

The reporter who had asked the question was standing in the back, his black note pad in his hands, pen poised. The question hung in the air for quite a while as we just sat there deliberating about what we should say. I think we were in a bit of a fog.

The last three days had been intense. We had driven to a hastily arranged appointment at Klassen's Funeral Home.

We had never planned a funeral before, so the funeral director led us through a list of things that we needed to think
about. So much had to be done. I was exhausted. We tried
to keep it businesslike, but the grief was unbearable.

I will never forget going into the huge display room filled
with coffins. A white coffin caught our attention almost immediately, one with a little pink bud embedded in ribboned
material. It was feminine ... almost childlike, yet adult.

This is surreal, I kept thinking. *This can't be happening.*
Candace will suddenly show up and tell us to stop this nonsense.
But it was real. We continued planning. Now that the search
was over, we seemed to have new energy to focus on the
tasks at hand. This funeral was now important to us.

But driving home, as Cliff and I reviewed our decisions
regarding the memorial card and program details, we started
arguing. It got nasty.

The argument made us all the more worried that we
were heading for some kind of emotional disaster. For me, it
was a sign that we were indeed heading for the same trauma
as our ten o'clock stranger, except for me it was something
I called the abyss.

I knew about this abyss. I had intimate knowledge of it.

I had been around the age of thirty when I had faced my
first real abyss—my madness—which I came to recognize
as a shapeless, chaotic mass inside of me. It was nothingness
filled with something dark, watery, and deep.

At that time, we were living in the small town of North
Battleford, Saskatchewan. Cliff had just accepted a position
as pastor of a small church, and I thought I finally would

be free to pursue my dreams. Since I had supported him through college, it was now my turn to finish university. But I hadn't counted on having children; we had two little girls who needed my full attention.

Suddenly I was overwhelmed with a sadness that I didn't understand. I had everything to make me happy—a wonderful husband, two delightful children—but I could barely get through my days, the burden of it all unbelievable.

My abyss would not be denied. I felt trapped—not so much by my husband or children but by what had led me to this vulnerable place, so unprepared for the challenges of being a mother. At thirty years old, I was stuck. Having moved around the country in the pursuit of my husband's dream and now living in a new community, I felt trapped at home without any social supports in place. It was as if all the trauma of my younger years was coming back to haunt me again. Throw in a little postpartum depression, and I knew I was in a dangerous place.

It was the abyss. I felt I was going to suffocate. It was not only an empty, chaotic space but also a hungry darkness; I felt the sadness licking at my feet.

The only way I could deal with it was to sneak out late at night when my family was sound asleep—safe—and get into our car and race across the prairie—that wide open space that went on and on. I just needed to feel as if I were flying. After an hour of that, I needed to drive down to the river and drive along the narrow roads next to the river's edge that snaked through the hills where it was quiet and dark—much like the abyss that was inside of me.

"Let go," I must have told myself a million times.

"Don't hang on!" I told myself. "Let it go. Forgive them all."

The term *forgive* derives from "to give" or "to grant," as in "to give up." To me, it has always meant giving up my right to do what comes naturally and to deliberately choose what my response will be. Sometimes the outcome is the same, but the process is different. Most often, that pause of giving up or letting go and then choosing another way can bring astonishing new results.

"Let the past go. Find something new."

Those words had launched me into an entirely new direction that gave me energy. I started to freelance as a feature writer for the local newspaper. At the end of our stay at North Battleford, I had somehow managed to let it go. I had conquered my depression and was excited about my life.

However, ever after I had developed a fear of the abyss.

Now the reporter's question was hanging in the air: "And what about the person who murdered your daughter?"

Cliff, my husband, was the first to answer it. And he said it with a kind of fait-accompli assurance. "We forgive."

I would do the only thing I knew how to do; I would let go. But this time I was facing an abyss more challenging and dangerous than the one I had escaped before. My quick heart check didn't allow me that confidence. I didn't know if my heart was letting go at the moment.

All I could feel was the breaking of a wounded mother's bleeding heart. I envied my husband's confidence; I still do. But I am a reluctant forgiver—a determined but reluctant forgiver who needs a lot of time. We didn't even know what that would mean.

I answered honestly. "I want to forgive."

The lights that had dimmed had come back on as they asked us what forgiving meant. I have no idea how we answered them. But to me it felt like I had dissolved into a conversation with friends as Cliff and I began to explore the concept with them.

I was stunned the next day that our choice and our attitude was what had grabbed the attention of the city. I had thought the stories would focus on the murder. They didn't. The articles highlighted our statement of forgiveness.

After the funeral, we were again shocked as the newspaper headlines—both papers, front page—jumped out at us. "Peace Triumphs!" said the *Winnipeg Sun,* which devoted the first four pages to our story. The story in the *Winnipeg Free Press* centered on Candace. Both suggested that somehow, in all of this tragedy, good had triumphed.

Dad had been unusually quiet with us, and I hadn't been sure if it was just the hustle and bustle or if he was troubled. I watched his reactions carefully as he read the stories. When he laid down the paper, a new peace was on his face.

"Now I understand," he said quietly. "On the train trip here, I was so puzzled. I wondered how God could allow something like this to happen. But now I know."

Chapter 3

THE EMOTIONAL LANDMINES

Life is an adventure in forgiveness.

—NORMAN COUSINS

The fashion models in their designer clothes were lined up and ready to walk the runway. Our own kindergarten-aged son had been stylishly dressed and was going to be part of the show. A local radio personality at the time was there to host the event. It was sold out.

But something was wrong—desperately wrong. I didn't know what was bothering me, but it was all wrong. I wondered if I should stop everything and sort it out. But everyone else was happy, and it was a smashing success. *The show must go on!* I told myself.

At the time, I was chair of the Child Find Manitoba chapter that we had begun even while Candace was missing so that we could access all the resources of the organization that was already in existence in other provinces. We wanted to get the word out about missing children easily and quickly, as soon as they were reported. This fashion show was a fundraising event organized by the board and made up of talented, beautiful women who were doing what they knew best.

But my soul wasn't in it.

One of the board members, kind and lovely, came up beside me. "What's wrong?"

I started describing my feelings. I don't even know what I said.

Then she said something: "We aren't looking for Candace anymore. She was found, Wilma."

I gasped. She had hit the nail on the head. I could feel the impact of her words.

Those seven weeks of looking for Candace had so traumatized me that I was locked into that time period. I couldn't move on. I could not enter into success.

I went through the motions of the evening as graciously as I could.

That night I wrote my resignation letter. I had some homework to do. The abyss was manifesting itself in negative ways that I hadn't even recognized.

I needed to explore my issues and deal with them. At the same time, I had been receiving calls from a support group organized mainly for parents of murdered children. The few conversations that I had with the president had been so informative and reassuring that I was intrigued. Because his own children had been murdered, he seemed to understand exactly what I was going through.

Eventually I joined the group. At the time we were meeting in a rather unique church, an old converted house on Notre Dame, which was a perfect setting for us—casual, a little chaotic, but homey.

That first meeting I felt as if I had entered a different

dimension. For one thing, we were all headliners. The murders of our children had put us on the front page of the newspapers. Second, instead of talking about our friends and family, we talked about the police as if they were friends of ours. We compared notes about the lawyers, judges, and psychologists. We were connected to all the organizations and agencies in the city but didn't belong to any of them. We could cry one moment and rant the next.

The first circle question was: "Do you feel you are going crazy?"

"Yes." We all agreed. It felt as if we were going crazy.

What made this group especially interesting to me was how articulate people were when it came to describing the "violation" of our lives. Most of us had led rather conventional lives before the event. We had lived by the book and had prided ourselves in doing things right. Then, without warning, our children had been targeted and murdered.

Suddenly we were thrown into a situation about which we had no background, no understanding, and no grid. Something had happened to us that we couldn't understand— and neither did anyone else.

Just listening to each other assured us that we were not going crazy. We met every other week just to be reassured of that over and over.

At the same time, there was a growing interest in trauma, restorative justice, and providing victim services. So it seemed, at least for me, that I was constantly being asked by other organizations what it was like to be a parent of a murdered child. Why did we meet? What were we learning? The underlying question was: What do victims need?

We didn't have the Internet or any search engines back then, so we didn't have access to all the information. Without much further thought, probably because of my journalism training, I became an amateur social researcher.

I would listen to the issues during the meeting and then go home at night and list them. As my list grew, I started to share them with the group and with my growing audience of churches and programs, including restorative-justice initiatives who wanted to hear my story. This elicited more stories from my audiences. I finally started to see the patterns and the design, and I grouped them together.

As I traveled across the country and met other people who have experienced the murder of a loved one, I would listen to their stories, and I started to incorporate their issues as well, distributing them into a list of fifteen issues that we faced. Except they weren't ordinary issues—these were issues of monstrous proportion, much bigger and fiercer than the ones I faced in my abyss of depression. These were monsters that attacked our most vulnerable places.

Each one of these monsters had the ability to pull us down and bury us in our own emotions so we couldn't move. There was no doubt that they were out to destroy us—mind, heart, body, and spirit—leaving nothing intact. When I wasn't fighting for my life, I was exhausted. No wonder I felt stuck.

What I had discovered in my first journey into the abyss is that the only way to deal with it was to face it and feel all the pain so I could identify and understand it. I couldn't go around it, over it, or under it; I had to go through it.

Now I was facing monsters I had never encountered, and I wasn't the only one. It seemed helpful to other crime victims to name and describe these monsters so that they could do battle better.

I could list them here very clinically, but I sometimes learned more about the abyss and its monsters by going to the movies than I did from doing research on trauma and the aftermath of murder.

Monster #1 resembles the catastrophe of the tower of Babel. It attacks our narrative. One minute we are communicating easily with everyone around us, the next minute there is a violent explosion in the middle of our lives, and thereafter no one is speaking the same language. Words are lost, vocabulary has changed, conflicts are rampant, pieces of information are lost, and the personal narrator has been silenced. Communication is gone.

Monster #2 resembles the eye of Dark Lord Sauron, who whispers, "You cannot hide. . . . I see you. . . . There is no hope for you—and I will destroy." It is hard to function normally under the grip of the eye. It keeps us spellbound and immobilized with terror.

Monster #3 acts like the Dementors straight out of the Harry Potter series, a negative, emotional energy force that feeds on our peace, hope, and happiness. Everyone else seems to be able to live at high speed, but we are drained of all energy, slowing down to first gear (and even that is hard to sustain). When unresolved grief has no place to be buried, it wanders like a zombie, pursuing the living for its energy.

Monster #4 is the Tasmanian Devil that comes roaring into the scene mirroring the turmoil inside us. Life makes no sense anymore. We spin and swerve out of control. Our psyche panics as it desperately tries to find answers to soothe the crazed mind.

Monster #5 comes at us like a rogue wave on the high seas of life. We are caught in the perfect storm. We try to power over it, but the wave starts to break, and we capsize— sinking into a spiritual blackness. Our old faith doesn't survive. It dies; it has to die to be reborn as something new.

Monster #6 is the evil stepmother, Lady Tremaine, who takes over our lives. We are sidelined, cursed, disgraced, completely diminished, stigmatized, and marginalized, so we are forced to find a small place beside the hearth in the ashes of life. Everyone else can go to the ball but us.

Monster #7 is the Führer himself at the helm of the concentration camp, brutally plundering and imprisoning everyone. We have encountered the spirit of the Nazi regime. Our space is no longer ours. We are prisoners. We don't have a name; we now have a number.

Monster #8 is like being caught in the trenches of a Transformer super power battle. We can't seem to identify what is evil and what is good.

Monster #9 is like a chill that sweeps into the room, and we know it is Lucifer, better known as the father of lies, the master of illusions, the artist of smoke and mirrors. This monster turns everyone around us into liars. We need the truth desperately.

Monster #10 is the birth of the green Hulk. Our emotions enlarge inside of us, outgrowing who we are as we become unrecognizable to those around us and to ourselves in our green rage.

Monster #11 erodes our moral sensibilities. Everyone seems fairly sane till they turn from a Dr. Jekyll into a Mr. Hyde. We meet people who live in different realities and interpret things differently from the way we do. We never know who will show up.

Monster #12 is like an elephant in the room. The systems and organizations that come in to help us can feel huge and imposing, which can feel limiting and dangerous when they start to move.

Monster #13 is the icy White Witch of the North in the Narnia series, who forces us to live in the land of endless winter during her reign. Even Christmas, the best part of winter, is prevented from ever coming. Years can slip by between words and healings, and in no time we have wasted ten years in the winter and missed every Christmas. It is the reign of endless waiting.

Monster #14 can be like a trickster or a joker, a seemingly jolly, harmless person who starts to entertain us, promising laughter and good times. We think we are engaging in joy and the promise of happiness until we realize we are up against the joker, a goofy clown who turns into a vicious, calculating, psychopathic killer at the end. There is no program, no medical plan. All the promises of healing lead to a dead end.

Monster #15 lives in the dark. Unexpectedly, we come face to face with the most sinister living creature, Shelob, the great spider in the caves of *The Lord of the Rings*, who has set out her net to catch and immobilize us to live without feeling—our world paralyzed. We are stuck. It is our worst nightmare.

Meeting just one of these monsters would be enough to defeat us, but to meet most or even all fifteen of them at the same time had me reeling. When I looked closely at the man who came to visit us the night Candace's body was found, I found traces of these fifteen monsters plaguing him.

My husband called it a list from hell. I called it the face of the worst kind of abyss—a hungry abyss filled with monsters who wanted to destroy us.

I had thought these monsters were unique to experiencing murder until I went to Happy Valley, Goose Bay, Labrador. After presenting the list to a crowd of community members who felt victimized, they asked me if this list could also apply to racial problems and other experiences. We sat down and compared notes. Yes, we decided. As a people, they were experiencing the same trauma we had.

After presenting them to a Sunday school, someone asked, "Can these apply to divorce?" We went through the list again and compared them. Yes.

Since then I've seen them applied to the trauma of discovering one's spouse has been unfaithful, church splits, and natural deaths. Actually, anything that has any traumatic impact can probably cause these monsters to appear.

Our first instinct is to do hand-to-hand battle with

these monsters, wanting to defeat them honorably. But the monsters are too big and overpowering. We have to accept that some forces are just too big for us to handle, so we forego. We let go—much like a cancer patient decides it is better to forego a breast or undergo chemotherapy, we need to chop off whatever limb the monster has won. It is a heart-wrenching decision. It demands a sacrifice. We do this in order to avoid being destroyed entirely.

But this is when we run into another problem.

When we start working toward inner healing, we realize the monsters have created an internal fragmentation in us. This becomes more noticeable when we start to forgive. I hear it a lot.

"I thought I had forgiven, but when this happened, it felt as if I hadn't forgiven at all."

"It's just not that simple. Our lives have been shattered."

"I've tried to forgive, but it keeps coming back."

"I want to forgive, but he needs to be held accountable."

"I want to forgive, but she keeps bullying me so that I can't just forget it all."

Internal fragmentation runs along our internal fault lines, which are our four temperaments: mind, heart, body, and spirit. Given that our world fragments and that our inner psyche fragments, I have calculated that the fifteen monsters multiplied by four comes to a total of sixty different fragmented pieces that need to come together.

Like Humpty Dumpty, it's not easy to put us back together. It takes work, many disciplines, and a lot of time. It might simply mean that one part of us has forgiven but another part hasn't. Our heart might forgive, so we might be able to greet the people who have wronged us quite pleasantly at a party. But our minds can't forgive, instead processing every tiny hurt again, cycling through it over and over.

Authors throughout history—from Hippocrates to the trendy personality types of our day—separate us into four parts. But the simplest way to understand our four temperaments was introduced to me by an elder. He showed us a chart of the mind, heart, body, and spirit. Could we identify the four in our lives?

Then he took it to another level.

"Where do you live?" he asked us.

"Do you live in your mind? Are you known as a thinker?"

"Do you live in your heart? Are you emotional and value relationships?"

"Do you live in your body? Do you like to be on the move?"

"Do you live in your spirit? Have you been called a dreamer?"

Where we live will probably determine how we respond to a situation and which of the fifteen monsters has gained control.

I am relational, so the night when Candace went missing, I was desperate—calling friends crying, and praying. It was only at ten o'clock that night when my other two children were whimpering that I realized I hadn't thought to eat or to feed them.

When I thought about the murderer, I found it easy to

think of meeting him, talking to him—but in my mind I fantasized about killing him. I couldn't sing "It is well with my soul" in church. I found intimacy difficult.

My husband, on the other hand, who lives in his mind, found it easy to say he chose to forgive and to put it out of his mind willfully, but then found anger management problems in his heart. He was furious with every minister we encountered, and his body developed kidney problems.

In many different places and ways in the Bible, we are told to love with all of our heart, all of our mind, all of our body, and all of our spirit. Different words were used at different times, but it comes down to the recognition and understanding that we live in four parts and need to achieve a four-part harmony to truly enter into forgiving as a complete person. It isn't that we can't forgive or that we haven't forgiven, we just haven't finished forgiving as the issues continue to present themselves to us.

In order to become integrated again and to repair the damage the monsters have done, we need to go through the processes of forgiveness. The first step in all of the processes is acceptance.

Acceptance is a person's assent to the reality of a situation. This is the beginning of surrendering to the brokenness. Acceptance breaks through the denial and the other games we play with ourselves when we want to avoid a loss or avoid facing the severity of a situation.

It isn't easy to accept the reality of the fact that something is over. The marriage partner is gone and isn't going to come back. If a girl is raped, her virginity is lost. A life taken is a life over. It can't be replaced. A city is bombed, and the country is never the same. Being fired means employment and all of what that meant is gone. When the money has been stolen, it won't be recovered.

Acceptance is that dreadful realization that no amount of banging on a door that has been closed for good is going to change anything. It's the realization that precious energy and time is being wasted as we fight a costly battle that we aren't going to win.

Accepting means letting it go. It is the first "let go"; there are more to come.

It seems that until we have closed the door, even nailed it shut and deliberately turned around, we can't see anything but the closed door.

Because this one process is so difficult, I have devoted most of this book to it.

Chapter 4

THE WAY

*Before you can live, a part of you has to die.
You have to let go of what could have been,
how you should have acted and what you wish
you would have said differently. You have to
accept that you can't change the past experiences,
opinions of others at that moment in time or
outcomes from their choices or yours. From this
point you will finally be free.*

—SHANNON L. ALDER

There were no leads in the case after Candace was found murdered, so I was surprised when a reporter called me a few months after her body was found.

"Have you heard the police's new theory of what happened to Candace?"

"No," I answered. Sometimes it seemed as if we were the last to hear.

Apparently, during the police's weekly press conference, they had made an announcement that they were establishing a reward for any clue leading to the arrest of Candace's murderer. The sergeant inspector had said that they suspected that "the motive didn't start off as murder. This offense may have started out as an innocent event. However, due to unknown circumstances, the victim was left in the shed, and, as a result, died of hypothermia."

When he was asked if the tragedy may have been the fallout of a childish prank gone awry, he said, "That's what I'm leading to."

He had gone on to say that murder motives usually include revenge or hate as well as personal, sexual, or financial gain. "The usual motives have been ruled out at this point in the investigation."

It was the word *innocent* that knocked the wind out of me.

"What do you think, Mrs. Derksen?" the reporter asked.

Innocent. I knew it wasn't innocent. I could feel myself starting to tremble. How did I know? How could I feel so strongly the terror that she must have gone through when no one else seemed to know? Why did I identify with that terror so strongly?

Then I remembered.

It had happened when I was in seventh grade. The day had been beautiful, the perfect temperature. My parents had gone to attend my older sister's graduation, and I had been left to look after my younger brother. To pass the evening, I set up our high-jumping stand and began to practice. I felt light on my feet—not enough to break any records, but light enough to really enjoy jumping over the makeshift bar.

I was thrilled when two neighbor boys passed the house on their bikes a few times and then finally had enough courage to stop. I had grown up with the younger boy and had a sister-brother relationship with him. But the other boy was fifteen and relatively new to the neighborhood, and he had the longest, darkest eyelashes I had ever seen. I thought he was wonderful.

I invited them to join me, but they couldn't jump. I don't remember exactly how it started, but as the evening shadows lengthened romantically, they threatened to kiss me. When I resisted, they started to chase me.

I was probably more confused than afraid at first. After all, it was only two boys—one was a childhood chum, and the other was a little shy.

I remember running barefoot through the garden, screaming and jumping with the greatest of ease over Mom's enormous potato plants as the boys lumbered after me. It took little effort to elude their grasp. At one point, I dashed into the house, but they followed me. I ran into the washroom and locked the door. But the younger one knew where we conveniently hung the key, and he started to open the door. I had no choice. I squirmed through the laundry chute into the laundry room and out the clothesline door. But the older one was there waiting for me. They had trapped me.

Half of me wanted them to catch me; the other half wanted them to leave me alone.

Together, they tied me to an apple tree.

I wasn't screaming anymore. The minute they overpowered me, they had ceased to be friends. I was scared.

After conferring, they turned to me. "If you kiss us, we'll set you free. If you don't, we'll dunk your head in the ditch until you say yes."

By *ditch*, they meant the sewer canals that ran along the houses and road. We loved to catch minnows in the ditches, but there were suspicious-looking brownish globs that accumulated along the edges. To have my head stuck in that—! But the choice was easy. I would never kiss them now. Never!

"I don't care," I told them. "You can drown me, and I'll never kiss you." I think that's when they realized they had gone too far, and I would never voluntarily give in. Unbeknownst to them, I had wiggled my hands until the ropes were free, and I ran into the house and locked all the doors.

That incident had started off as an innocent prank, but it had gotten out of hand. The minute they overpowered me, it had lost its innocence, it had ceased to be a prank. It had ceased to be fun. And the minute it lost its innocence, I had stopped screaming and struggling; I had become frightened. Whatever feelings I'd had for the older boy had died instantly.

So I knew what the police meant when they said it could have started innocently, but I had to disagree. It was a pleasant winter day, and the placing of her friends just didn't fit into an innocent prank gone wrong.

The day had been too uncomfortable for anything to have just developed lazily on its own. There had to have been a strong motive already in place before Candace came on the scene. She wouldn't have hung around for any kind of nonsense; she knew we were waiting for her, and none of the people who mattered to her were even in the vicinity. Whatever had happened never had any shred of innocence about it.

I wanted to scream! Candace had been forcibly taken to a strange place. Couldn't the police see the difference? She had been forced! They were trying to say, whether they meant to or not, that the victim was in some way responsible.

"Mrs. Derksen?" The reporter was waiting for an answer.

I took a deep breath. "We can't make light of the fact that she was tied up and left to die. If it was intended as a prank, something went wrong. I still believe it was a malicious prank." The word *"prank"* was my one concession to the police statement as I tried to minimize the distance between our opinions.

Even though we learned later that the press conference was a police ploy to flush out the killer, which didn't work, it was the last public story. It was what everyone would remember for the next twenty-three years.

At the end of every one of my presentations, it seemed someone would ask, "And how do you know it wasn't a prank?" Not that it would have made much difference to my journey at that time, but I could feel the attempt to minimize murder. There is nothing more painful than the dishonor of minimization.

It was one thing to forgive the offender—whoever he was. It was another thing to forgive the police and the ongoing minimization of what happened in the shed.

"Let it go," I reminded myself as I brushed off the questions.

I'll never forget the visit of another stranger who began to give me the courage to talk about forgiveness in a new way.

I received a simple email. "I'm a writer in New York.... I would love to come to Winnipeg and interview you for a book I'm writing. I have been reading the story of your daughter and have been very moved by it. I don't know if you are still giving interviews, but if you are, do let me know. I would be happy to come to Winnipeg. Cheers, Malcolm Gladwell."

As I stared at the name, I remembered that some time ago I had found myself in Chapters bookstore with some time to waste, so I meandered around the display tables. There was one table in the front of the store that seemed to draw me, and on that table was one book in particular entitled *The Tipping Point* that had caught my eye. I picked it up, sat in a nearby chair, and skimmed through it. It held me and inspired me. The writer immediately became my hero.

I wrote back simply. "Are you the author of *The Tipping Point*?"

"Yes." He then went on to describe his latest project. It was going to be a book with the working title *David and Goliath*. He said he wanted to talk about our choice to forgive.

Of course I said yes.

The doorbell rang on the morning he said he would come. It was him. I was so excited. Since he didn't want anything to eat, I took two bottles of water and we went to sit in our gazebo in our backyard garden.

It was obvious from the start that he had studied me. He

knew exactly where my father had been the entire time during Candace's disappearance. He had seen my TEDx talk and my Bill C-10 presentation to the government. It just seemed he knew everything about me. I was astounded that anyone of such importance would take the time to study me.

I actually have little memory of what we talked about, but it was as if I were talking to a longtime friend. It was a beautiful conversation, something I will always treasure.

"Can you tell me something?" His eyes were dancing mischievously. "When you announced to the world during that first press conference that you would forgive ... did that public declaration hold you accountable? Were there times when you were forced to live up to it even when you didn't feel like it?"

It was the first time I had thought of it in that way—the importance of others in holding us on track, the track that we chose for ourselves.

"Yes," I said. There was so much relief in admitting that.

Forgiveness is a little like marriage. We fall in love and then declare our love to everyone, but it is only after that public ceremony that we really find out what it means to live up to that commitment. During those tough times when it is tested, that invisible audience helps us stay true.

As all good conversations do, they also teach us something of ourselves.

Perhaps most revealing for me was Gladwell's interest in my Mennonite roots and how they influenced our decision to forgive. From early on I had learned that forgiveness was a viable option. I had learned that it wasn't a miracle drug to mend all broken relationships but a process that demanded patience, creativity, and faith. It demanded humility and a deep love for each other.

My Mennonite roots had given me a long list of historical examples of forgiveness dating as far back as the sixteenth century, when the Mennonites were founded on Menno Simon's first act of forgiveness. I was steeped in the belief.

What brought it all together for me was a simple novel by Lloyd C. Douglas called *White Banners*, which explored the same philosophy of forgiveness that I had grown up with but was more accessible to me as a woman. The historical forgiveness themes of my culture were mainly male oriented, addressing war, persecution, and aggressive behavior. I needed something more subtle, relational, and geared toward ordinary family issues.

The main plot of this book was about a woman named Hannah who drifted into the lives of the Ward family in a small Indiana town in 1919. Hannah makes herself useful as a cook and housekeeper and stays with the Wards, but her real interest is in meeting their neighbor, teenager Peter Trimble. It turns out that Peter is the son she bore out of wedlock and gave up for adoption, and now Hannah has returned to town to see what sort of young man her son has become.

The subplot is how Hannah's first love, Phillip, a wealthy idealist, explores the idea of nonresistance but dies before he can test his theories. Because Hannah remains in love with him, she actually tries to live out his ideals in her own life as a kind of experiment. The best part of the book was that the author set the drama of her decision to live Phillip's strange creed in a woman's setting, dealing with housekeeping issues, a mother's issues, and even business issues—the three settings that challenged me.

It all sounded immensely romantic and idealistic—especially the part about it being an experiment.

Hannah's conversations about forgiveness intrigued me:

"You mean it would do something to me on the inside; something that would flavor all my thoughts and actions?"

"Exactly! You've said it. It is the secret renunciation, the giving-up, the letting-go, the sacrifice that nobody understands but the person who does it—that generates inside of you a peculiar power to—"

"To do what?"

"To do almost anything you like …"

Way back then, I decided that I wanted to be a Hannah.

After Candace disappeared, as I huddled in our basement in the middle of the night facing the first onslaught of the monsters emerging out of the darkness of the abyss, my mentor was Hannah. It was all about *secret renunciation, the giving-up, the letting-go.*

"Letting go" became my mantra.

I had just given my presentation at the Model United

Nations Leadership Conference in Qatar on "The Road Less Traveled: Forgiveness in Leadership" when three promising young men came up to ask me a question.

I had been briefed to be free about my stories about forgiveness but not to appear to be promoting a foreign faith.

The young men planted themselves in front of me. "Do we need to have faith to forgive?" I knew this was extremely important. Their eyes were wide open.

Because it was a question that kept coming up—especially when I visited penitentiaries—I had spent some time thinking about it. Faith had been essential to my understanding of forgiveness, along with hope and love. There is that verse "and now these three remain: faith, hope and love. But the greatest of these is love" that had crystallized in my mind.

I took a deep breath. "Yes, you do."

Their eyes narrowed.

"But there are all kinds of belief systems," I told them.

For some it might be the belief that "what goes around comes around."

For some it might take on the shape of karma.

For some who rely on authority figures, it might be the belief in a person or a leader.

For some it is a higher power.

For someone to find the strength to forgive, I am uncertain it matters what the brand, what the origin, or what the size; in this instance, the thing that matters is that the faith has to be our own. One would think it would take a lot of faith to produce tall oak trees, but in reality it starts with a tiny acorn. Faith could start even smaller than that—a tiny, almost invisible mustard seed.

It doesn't have to be much of a faith. Even chimpanzees can forgive and make up after a misunderstanding, much like humans do. Even a child can understand forgiveness and learn it. So no matter who we are or what our fundamental beliefs are, it is possible. We need to believe in the end result. Faith is "confidence in what we hope for and assurance about what we do not see."

So I told the young men that faith is necessary in forgiveness. They seemed to be able to accept my explanation. I heard later it had been hotly discussed. Apparently that was a good thing.

And yes, I do believe that we all have the ability to forgive. I do believe that forgiveness will grow in every garden.

The unfortunate thing about forgiveness is that it isn't native to our land. We do have to plant it and activate it by watering it and paying special attention to it. We have to have faith that it will grow. And once activated, it needs to grow through use. It is tiny at first but grows each time we step out in faith.

After a presentation, someone inevitably will come to me with genuine compassion in their eyes, often in tears, and ask, "How do I help my friend to forgive?" At those moments I wish I had a magic wand to give them because there is no quick fix. It is a process—and sometimes a very long one.

Sometimes it will take a lifetime to forgive one incident. However, the beginning of the process begins with accepting what has happened to us. Accepting is the first "let go," and there are many more to come.

Even though I can't personally promise anything, I can point to another person much better prepared and able. For this journey, we need the perfect companion and mentor not only to give us the right words but also to hold our hands as we stumble along this new path—someone who has also gone the distance.

There is just such a person. A long time ago, there was a Nazarene who preached forgiveness, taught forgiveness, lived forgiveness, and in the end went the distance, ultimately dying for the cause.

As the perfect teacher, he found the perfect setting to introduce us to the way of forgiveness and letting go. Overlooking the Sea of Galilee, he sat on the edge of a mountain, a natural amphitheater with perfect acoustics so everyone below could hear him. There he spoke to his chosen audience, the common folk who were following him, so that his message would be understandable to them and thereby to everyone—even us. Understanding it isn't the problem; living it out is the challenge.

There, on the top of a rock with the sea breeze fanning his face, he put words to the radical way of living out forgiveness. Poetically and courageously, he outlined the way of letting go.

Even back then, everyone knew his audacious message was actually the very antithesis of everything being taught in the culture of the day. With his words, this peasant Nazarene literally crashed head-on not only into their systems but into ours as well. To this day his words are well known for their poignancy and conciseness, for their sheer poetry, for their morality and practicality. He wasn't a powerful person in the community at that time, but his words were.

People have called it a counterintuitive sermon and one that is impossible to live up to. True, it is confrontational, bold, and stark. It needed to be. It is the greatest teaching ever given. It was a rather long, complicated sermon, but underlying his words was this simple message: There is a way of life—there is an authentic, deep, alternative way of life—that you must live if you want to be free of this world's brokenness.

Back then the world needed a new script, and he gave it to them, even as he continues to give it to us. Letting go was his idea in the first place. And in him I found the courage and the faith to let go. I had no idea how many things he would ask me to let go of. There were fifteen, to be exact.

Chapter 5

Letting Go of the Happy Ending

> Forgiveness is the only way to reverse the
> irreversible flow of history.
>
> —Hannah Arendt

Two uniformed police officers knocked on our door at approximately eleven o'clock the night Candace disappeared.

Instead of taking one of our photos of Candace as I expected and rushing out the door, they sat back, relaxed, and watched us closely. They wanted to know what kind of parents we were. What was our relationship with Candace like? Had we argued with her? Was she upset that I hadn't picked her up?

We pulled out all the stops. We thought that if anything would immediately impress on them our solid family values, integrity, and love, it would be our Christian commitment.

The more outspoken officer perked up and said, "I know what the problem is."

We both straightened. "What?"

"You," he answered, glancing at both of us.

"What do you mean *us?*"

He spelled it out. "You're both religious, and Candace is rebelling."

How incredibly naive we'd been! I wouldn't normally have cared about their skepticism, but our daughter's life depended on whether they believed us. We had to convince them. We told them that Candace would never have run away because she was expecting her best friend to come and visit us the next day.

"Is she religious?" the officer asked.

"Who, Candace?"

"No, her friend." I could see where he was going. So I said nothing and just nodded. It seemed as if my moody silence was answer enough for him.

"Are the friend's parents religious?" he probed.

According to his definition, yes, they would be perceived as religious too, so I nodded.

"You see, that proves my point. Maybe Candace is rebelling against your whole religious community." I was horrified.

One minute we are communicating easily with everyone around us, people believe what we are saying, and the facts are convincing. Suddenly something happens—a crime— and there are incredible invisible barriers to communication. Words are lost, vocabulary changes, dissension arises, pieces go missing, arguments break out easily, and one's own narrative has become a critic. This is very disconcerting, because the words we choose are incredibly important to us. For example, the police officers were calling it a runaway case. We were acting out of our own word, *abduction*. One acts very differently when it is a runaway case versus when it is a stranger abduction, when it is an accident versus criminal negligence, when it is consensual sex versus a rape.

The word we choose is extremely important because the healing in our story can't begin to happen until we've faced the right words that identify the reality before us.

When Candace's body was found seven weeks later, our story went noticeably from "missing" to "murder." By using this word, they were changing the story, and I didn't like the new one they were creating.

When betrayed, violated, or assaulted, we feel completely fragmented and undone. The worst part is that we also lose our ability to find words to describe in a cohesive way what happened at that critical time. We can even lose our ability to call for help or withstand the investigation that feels like an inquisition. There are simply not enough words in our vocabulary for those moments.

Yet the need to tell our story and express ourselves is there from the moment we are born. We build our lives on words. We have an inside narrator—perhaps even a few—who constantly gives us words. Whether we feel in control of our story or our story is in control of us, the story demands words and demands to be told. Words carry immeasurable importance to us. The universe was created with a word, Jesus healed with a word, and politicians have risen and fallen from power over their use of words. Our world is limited by our words.

Finding our own words for what happened is our way of healing and becoming integrated again.

Sitting on the edge of the mountain addressing the crowd, the Nazarene says, "You are the light of the world. A town built on a hill cannot be hidden. Neither do people light a lamp and put it under a bowl. Instead they put it on its stand, and it gives light to everyone in the house. In the same way, let your light shine before others, that they may see your good deeds and glorify your Father in heaven."

As victims, when our stories are in tatters, we are reluctant to climb onto a hill and let everyone see us. Yet that's what these words are saying. To "shine" as described here means we need to be transparent. We need to be telling the stories of our lives. That might be OK for some of us, but the only story we are able to tell is our stories of complaint. We don't think we have a "good deed" story. We don't have a story with a happy ending or even an ending at all. It's open and raw and unfinished.

The Greek translation of the word "good" is kalos, which means lovely, beautiful, helpful, honest, useful, and well adapted to its purpose or end. Originally, it referred to the beauty of form. With this word we can interpret "good deeds" to mean that we need to be shining forth a beautiful integrity before everyone—no matter what the story is—so that amongst the flaws they see our vulnerability.

But why should we do this? Why should we expose our

broken, unfinished, destroyed, vulnerable, and complicated stories?

The Nazarene is telling us not to hide under the bed because the story we tell ourselves initially isn't the final version of the story. In fact, our broken stories are beautiful opportunities for others to enter into our stories and identify with us. I remember one such incident that revealed for me the power of story—no matter the ending.

As a group of parents of murdered children, we were invited to a prison. We were so frightened. There were three of us, three storytellers: a father whose daughter had been murdered, a mother whose son had been murdered by his wife, and me. Our purpose was prevention—to tell them our stories so forcefully they would never want to hurt another person in their lives.

As those fierce prison doors clanged shut behind us, the people in the group looked a little worried.

At the last moment we were told that, because of the interest in the program, they had opened the meeting to the general prison population. The gym was full. To make things worse, just as we were about to enter, they also told us that the kingpin of the penitentiary had decided to attend.

Kingpin is an old term for the leader in the prison, known to be the worst of the population. Apparently, to gain this kind of status, he had also killed two men within the prison walls. He was pointed out to us sitting at the back of the room.

I told my story first, then there was a short break after my story. When we came back, we noticed that the kingpin had moved to the middle of the room and was sitting by the aisle.

This time the father told his story of finding his daughter raped and murdered. At group meetings he had always been a kind, churchgoing type of man; now, standing in front of the inmates, he started using language I had never heard before. He vented and didn't pull any punches.

After he was finished, the inmates began to tell their stories of how they too had experienced the murder of family members. I could sense that they were trying to portray themselves as victims. I knew this would not go over with our storytellers, and it didn't. When it was time for the third story, I was about to introduce the mother whose son had been murdered by his wife.

She shook her head. "I'm not telling my story to these men." I filled in time, hoping she would gain courage.

In response to something I said, the leader of an inmate organization stood up and said, "I know what is wrong with you and why you can't carry on with your lives. You carry your hatred and your dead children with you much like mother monkeys carry their dead babies. You just need to forgive."

Then the mother stood up. She was angrier than I had ever seen her. "I will never forgive," she said in a deep, other-worldly voice. The room fell deathly quiet. The air was tense. I felt the whole thing would turn into a riot. I was ready to throw myself between the victims and a bullet or knife or whatever could come flying.

Then the kingpin stood up. "It's okay. That's why we

are all in here, because we haven't been able to forgive either." And then he looked around the room. "Have we?" And there was a murmur of assent.

At that moment, the barrier between us and the offenders seemed to evaporate as the room became one. We were all offenders and victims trapped in anger and frustration. We were all facing injustices. We were all angry with our stories.

The mother then told her story. In her low voice, she commanded attention in a new way.

When our time was up and we had to leave, the kingpin moved to the front of the room, then I saw the father of the murdered child move cautiously toward him. Then he and the kingpin of the penitentiary shook hands, and it felt as if a new story had begun.

———

I had to let go of the need to find a happy ending
to my story. I had to let go of my perfect story—
and write the story that was happening to me.

———

Chapter 6

LETTING GO OF FEAR

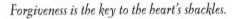

Forgiveness is the key to the heart's shackles.

—RICHARD PAUL EVANS

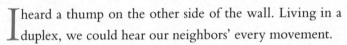

I heard a thump on the other side of the wall. Living in a duplex, we could hear our neighbors' every movement.

As Cliff went upstairs to check on the children, I saw one of our neighbors coming up the sidewalk. I opened the door and asked if I could speak to him.

We told him that our teenage daughter hadn't come home from school and asked him if he had noticed anything unusual. I watched carefully for his reaction. Would it be guarded? Did he know something?

He seemed immediately sympathetic and introduced himself as a wrestler from eastern Canada. He explained that he was staying with his wrestling buddies next door while he was training for a match the next weekend.

"If you need help," he said before he left, "if she's in trouble, just call me." Had I imagined it, or had I actually flexed his muscles ever so slightly?

Wrestlers—that explained the sound of bodies flying against the wall. How I wished that I could search their house.

I don't think I slept at all that night. I heard every start of the furnace, every snore, every deep breath on our side as well as on the other side of our duplex. Somewhere in the night I heard some dull thuds, and I wondered if it was Candace, bound and gagged, trying to get loose from a closet just on the other side of the wall.

Our neighbors started to stir unusually early the next morning, and I was down in the kitchen in a flash. I made some coffee and sat at our kitchen table so I could watch every movement in the backyard. A streetlight in the alley right behind our house was placed perfectly for my little stakeout.

Our neighbor couldn't have eaten much of a breakfast, because the back door opened at almost the same time as the kitchen light went on. I moved closer to the window, hiding in the shadows. For one desperate moment I wondered what would happen if he saw me. What if he suspected we knew who he was? Would our whole household be in danger?

The figure of a man stumbled down the sidewalk, shielding himself from the bitter cold. Just as he moved into the alley, he turned to look both ways and to look back at the house. The streetlight shone brightly on his face. I drew back from the window and went into the living room with my cup of coffee.

I was becoming obsessed with my fear. I could feel and hear everything. Fear of this magnitude can be overwhelming after a violent crime. I can only describe it as having a grizzly bear come to live in our house. I can assure you that when a grizzly bear rules the house, all normal living activity is put on hold. You can't sleep with a grizzly in the room, you can't eat, you can't have a good conversation, you can't digest properly, you can't read, you can't learn, you can't share an intimate moment with your partner. Life is frozen.

Fear grows. Even though fear is a normal emotion and even helpful in dangerous situations, it can quickly become a phobia. A phobia occurs when a fear is greatly exaggerated or the object of the fear is nonexistent. For example, it is only natural to be afraid of a pit bull with a reputation, but to be afraid of a sweet little purse dog on a leash is irrational.

According to Dr. Karl Albrecht, who is the author of *Feararchy*, there are only five basic fears, out of which almost all of our other so-called fears are manufactured. These fears are:

- Extinction—the fear of annihilation, of ceasing to exist.
- Mutilation—the fear of losing any part of our precious bodily structure.
- Loss of Autonomy—the loss of control of our destiny.
- Shunning—the fear of abandonment, rejection, and loss of connectedness.
- Egoism/Ego-death—the fear of humiliation, shame, or any other mechanism of profound self-disapproval.

As a family, we were facing all five—fear of death, fear of sexual assault, fear of murder, fear of being cursed, which would mean being rejected, shunned, humiliated, and unemployable.

Dr. Margee Kerr, who has often been referred to as a scare expert, has discovered through her research that if we have an underlying safety net, we have a great capacity to enjoy a scary situation. Fear can be a good experience. Fear responses flood our bodies with adrenaline, endorphins, and dopamine, which are exhilarating. So when fear is experienced in a safe place, fear promises us extraordinary exhilaration and intimacy. In other words, it makes us feel alive.

This puts an entirely different spin on the kind of terror trauma that we have been exposed to. The difference between good fear and destructive fear is that good fear has a safety net.

By next fall our lives had returned to normal ... or so I thought. Around the time I expected Odia to come home from school, I hovered around the front window.

I was relieved to see her coming down the sidewalk so content, so happy to see me. But I was also furious. She was alone. We had quite carefully arranged a neighborhood watch with the other mothers in the community to make sure our children never walked home alone.

Seeing my alarm, Odia told me that she had been a little slow putting on her jacket and hadn't walked home with her friends. She had told them to go on ahead. Being more of an introvert, she hadn't minded being alone after a school day. All I could think of was that she had disobeyed me. I lost it on her—I berated her until she cried.

"But nothing happened, Mom," she reassured me over and over again. She was safe at home. Why was I so angry? Why was I so fearful? I couldn't explain it to her; my fears were beyond words. I was so disappointed in myself. I had wanted to live beyond fear.

◀

The Nazarene shows he understands. It is a normal and natural response to be afraid. Surveying the crowd sitting so peacefully and trusting, the Nazarene continues. "Blessed are the poor in spirit, for theirs is the kingdom of heaven."

"Poor in spirit" may actually describe someone with a fearful, cowering disposition. It is contradictory that a royal citizen of a new kingdom would be characterized by fear— another word for trauma. As victims, we are well aware of how our cowering spirits can be a negative and destructive force in the victim community.

Is there something we are missing here? Is there a healthy fear? Notice the safety net in the verse. It is the kingdom of heaven.

What the Nazarene is trying to portray here is a new kingdom language. He is unashamedly presenting an entirely new order of living. He is actually an ambassador of another country, representing a separate realm of independent actions or controls, a counterintuitive lifestyle. He is also promising an elitist membership by explaining that belonging to this kingdom bestows privileges and rights to a citizenship and empowerment of the ruling authority—God. That is his answer to fear: a close relationship with the Creator of this world, the ultimate authority.

But it isn't easy to remain loyal to a kingdom that seems so obscure!

Shortly after Candace disappeared, most of the schools in our area introduced a "street proofing" program, and a trend began for having all the children fingerprinted. The Child Find organization was part of it. They were trying to teach the children the difference between a stranger and a neighbor.

It was a warm winter—almost spring—day. Our neighbor was working on a car in his back yard when he noticed us returning from a shopping trip. He called out a friendly greeting, "Hi there!"

I expected Syras to respond, but he was quiet.

Once inside the house, Syras got onto the kitchen table and looked out the kitchen window.

"Mommy," he asked, "is that man a neighbor or a stranger?"

This neighbor was the kind of person whom you would like to instinctively trust. His place was orderly. His dogs were under control and looked loved, and they had always been friendly. But in all honesty, we knew nothing about him. He was what one would consider the perfect neighbor–stranger.

But what did I want? Did I want my little son to trust everyone? I ached to take the safer route. I wanted to end all risks and pronounce this man a stranger.

Syras was waiting impatiently. "Come on, Mom. Is he a stranger?"

Syras didn't understand my tears when I hugged him as I lifted him off the table and put him down.

"No, sweetheart, he's not a stranger. He's actually a very nice neighbor. And the next time he says hi, the polite thing to do is to say hi back."

"Oh, I will," he said with a big sigh of relief.

He had gained a new freedom; I felt as if I had lost some of mine.

I had to remember the Nazarene's words. Privileged are they who deliberately discard that panic of self-preservation and fear and dare to live life on the edge for others. Our souls will ultimately be saved if we risk it all for love.

I had to let go of my fear and embrace
risk again, knowing that guaranteed
safety was now forever an illusion.

Chapter 7

LETTING GO OF MY GRIEF

Forgiving does not erase the bitter past. A healed memory is not a deleted memory. Instead, forgiving what we cannot forget creates a new way to remember. We change the memory of our past into a hope for our future.

—LEWIS B. SMEDES

I still remember that sunny day when Candace came into the kitchen where I was quickly stirring some cookie dough.

"Mom, I found *my* song, and I want you to hear it."

"Play it while I put these on the pan before they harden."

"No, I want you to listen. I'll wait."

She curled up on the chair to watch and nibble.

About a year and a half earlier, when Cliff had been in charge of music for a roller-skating night for young people, he had haunted the Christian music stores, bringing home all sorts of demonstration tapes. Of course, Candace had loved Cliff's new responsibility. She had helped him pick out songs that kids her age liked.

"Is it rock?" I asked.

"No, you'll like it. It's by Michael W. Smith." The name

didn't mean anything to me at the time. "It's a song that's just mine. I like the words and the music."

"What's it about?" I asked.

"Friends."

I had to smile. It was always about friends with her.

After the cookies were finished, I followed her into the living room and sat down. She put the tape on, and the song floated through the room. I tried hard to listen to the words. Though most of them escaped me, the theme was unmistakable. It was about the value of friends.

When the last note faded, she sat smiling smugly. "It's me, isn't it?"

I nodded.

A year and a half later, she was still playing the song as often as when she discovered it. We heard it every night before she went to bed.

After she disappeared, someone asked me what Candace was really like. I knew there was only one answer to that question. The tape was still beside the bed in my old battered tape recorder that Candace had claimed. I took it downstairs to play it. When the familiar beat began, it was as if Candace had walked into the room, swaying slightly to the music, the hint of a dreamy smile on her lips, that faraway, peaceful look in her eyes—totally absorbed in her music. "*Packing up the dreams God planted in the fertile soil of you …*"

The words filled the room. I thought the pain would rip me apart. It was a good-bye song! She had chosen a good-bye song! Had she known? Had she in some way chosen this song for us because she knew she was going?

Then the chorus:

> *And friends are friends forever*
> *If the Lord's the Lord of them.*

I sat stunned. The song unleashed all of my grief then—
and still does. Waves and waves of it over and over.

We played the song at the memorial, and tears rolled
unchecked. But out of the corner of my eye, I could see
the cameras in the wings. Police cars were outside. I knew
plainclothes policemen were at our house, guarding it and
probably inspecting it as well. I knew that the guest book
would be taken after the memorial so they would know
exactly who had attended. "The murderer always comes to
the funeral to see what an impact their actions had created,"
the police had told us.

Even as we mourned, there was never any doubt that we
were in the middle of a police investigation.

When there is an injustice involving murder or any such
loss, it is so much easier to concentrate on the justice issues
rather than to focus on that much less attractive emotion
of grief. Grief introduces us into a time of low energy—
waiting and resting, in which we need to do our mourning.

In the case of a crime, the persistent police investigation, media attention, offender presence, and public interest
can all threaten to overshadow the necessary grieving process. For example, in our grief support groups, the members
carried the pictures of those they had lost; we didn't. We
talked about the justice issues till eventually our inattention

to grief began to manifest itself in unhealthy ways. Others avoid mourning because it feels unacceptable or foreign.

I remember one group meeting when a father of a murdered son came to join us. He was rather disruptive right from the beginning, telling us that our group wasn't really effective. We should be doing something, not just sitting around and talking.

We weren't used to the anger, and we sat there stunned, agreeing with him. We should do more. But that didn't seem to appease him; he just continued railing against us. Finally, as a means of distracting him, we asked him about his son.

As the story unraveled, so did his emotions. He began to cry—to sob—and we comforted him with our stories. When the meeting was over, he was a changed man. His eyes were no longer dull and angry but shiny with new life and love.

Later we heard that even though he never came to another meeting, we had helped him immensely, and he became one of our greatest endorsers. That was when I learned the important healing power of tears and the grieving process.

When we have unresolved grief, we have unresolved emptiness in our lives, and a loss that can show itself in expressions of anger, compulsive hoarding, incessant talking, and such. We get stuck in the past.

After the funeral, we heard by a strange coincidence that Michael W. Smith, the singer of Candace's favorite song, was scheduled to appear at the Winnipeg Concert Hall. He called late one night saying that he had heard our story and wanted to give Heidi, Candace's best friend, and our family complimentary tickets to the concert. He also made arrangements for us to go backstage later to meet him. Odia, of course, thought this was pure heaven, but I dreaded it.

More than that, I was afraid. A concert by Michael W. Smith could push us over the edge. How could I possibly bear hearing her song live when I couldn't even listen to a scratchy, faded, recorded version without falling apart?

There was only one way. First thing on the morning of the concert, I put on the tape and forced myself to listen to "Friends Are Friends Forever." The song had not lost any of its ability to resurrect Candace's presence, and I could feel her come swaying into the room in time to the music with that bright smile that I had seen on her face every time she listened to her song.

I played it again and again and again, trying to substitute her memories with mine, hoping that by making it mine, her memory wouldn't be as painful. But I couldn't. It was her song. She had loved it so much and had played it so often that it was impossible for any of us to adopt it as our own. The hurt in that song would reach out and wrench my heart out of its cavity and squash it like mud.

I tried to treat it as background music as I dusted the house. But every time the chorus started, the dust would blur, and I'd start sobbing.

When Cliff came home, he took one look at me, marched into the living room, and turned it off. "What do you think you are doing?"

"I'm listening to it until I won't cry anymore."

He shook his head. "Don't you know that song will

always make us cry? You'll never get over it. Doing this will make you sick, and you have to go tonight."

It was making me sick.

Actually, it was a wonderful concert. And when Michael W. Smith sang the song, I cried—and so did everyone else. But it was dark, there were no cameras on us, and it was good to cry. Crying in a crowd helped.

There was a place for tears; there always would be. Thereafter, we could become comfortable and unapologetic about them.

Sitting on the edge of the mountain, the Nazarene notices a young widow at the edge of the crowd, eyes still brimming with endless tears. He says, "Blessed are those who mourn, for they will be comforted."

The original word for mourning combines the two words *grieving* and *mourning*. Grief is the emotional response. It means we feel. We are privileged to feel. Mourning is the process and often ritualized tasks of grieving.

In those days, the burial practices were a sacred tradition that reflected the significance of death. Death was central because it was considered a part of life—a reflection not only of sorrow but also of the great value placed on the individual's life.

A death in the family immediately caused grief and lamentation expressed in numerous forms. Among the first signs of grief and mourning was the obligatory tearing of garments. Then the deceased's body was washed and anointed with various oils and spices, wrapped in a unique linen cloth that contained spices and placed on a stone shelf that was carved into the bedrock wall of a tomb. After the body was prepared, it was carried to the cemetery in a procession of lamentation and grief, accompanied by professional wailers. Grief gave opportunity to express relationship, intimacy, and connection to gain comfort. The word *comfort* in the original language means that the mourners will be sought after. In other words, those who mourn, those with tears in their eyes, become attractive and even desirable in their vulnerability.

Working with our grief is important. William Worden, well-known author and researcher on grief, says there are four tasks of mourning, which I followed vaguely. We first must accept the reality of the loss. Then we need to work through the grief and feel the pain. After that, we need to adjust the environment around us to reflect the loss. We need to learn to live without the person we've lost. Finally, it is helpful to find creative ways to keep their memory alive while letting it go.

Tears are beautiful because they are an outward manifestation of a loving heart.

As victims, our natural impulse is to run away from the vulnerability of grieving. It is especially hard to grieve in the presence of a menacing enemy. However, if we don't enter into this vulnerability, we will be missing out on a profound opportunity to renew our spiritual connection to others.

The Nazarene is calling us to pause in the grief to gain wisdom and compassion. But it is a pause, not an end in itself. Grief can become a substitute for the lost life; just the simple act of being sad kept Candace close.

During that first year of intense grief, a friend of ours

took my daughter out for a treat. When they came back, I asked her how Odia was doing. "Your daughter said that she wished that she could have her old mom back again. I suppose you know what that means?"

Odia wanted me to be myself again. Couldn't I at least have one year to mourn? One year to be sad? But a year is a long time in a child's life, and my children couldn't wait. Adjusting meant giving up my tears and my sadness.

To help us be happy again, we decided to go to a circus. Even this simple act wasn't easy. Leaving the house that evening was tough. I dawdled until I was the last to close the door. I felt I was betraying Candace all over again. Our purpose for going out was solely to forget and to laugh.

At first it was sad—the obvious display of humor and the clowns were off-putting. For us in our state, they looked downright ugly. But then this huge elephant turned his big behind to us, waited, and then peed.

We howled with laughter. It was as if a dam had broken. We laughed and laughed, and after that, even the clowns were funny.

As we laughed, we realized we weren't denying our emotions of grief or our need for tears; we were embracing our need for laughter and for life. We couldn't deny the tears and sadness, nor could we deny the rest of life.

I had to let go of my grief and learn to laugh again. I had other children who needed me to concentrate on life, not death.

Chapter 8

LETTING GO OF MY EGO

When we think we have been hurt by someone in the past, we build up defenses to protect ourselves from being hurt in the future. So the fearful past causes a fearful future and the past and future become one. We cannot love when we feel fear.... When we release the fearful past and forgive everyone, we will experience total love and oneness with all.

—GERALD G. JAMPOLSKY

I had first seen Percy, the neighborhood alley cat, the spring of the year Candace disappeared. It had been warm that day, and there had been puddles in the driveway. For some reason I had decided to take all three kids shopping with me.

The kids stuck close to me in the store, where they wanted everything they saw, but it was another story when I drove into our driveway and wanted them to help me carry the grocery bags inside. They chose all the light bags and fled into the house before I could say anything.

While I was struggling to lift three of the heaviest bags and close the trunk at the same time, I looked up in time to see a horrible-looking black cat streak into our house between Syras's short legs. Instead of being alarmed, Odia quickly closed the door behind them.

I scrambled up the walk. There was a wild cat in our house with my children! I had visions of a wild black animal clawing up my drapes, hissing at the kids, and hiding behind the furniture never to come out again.

I burst into the kitchen. "Where's the—!" It wasn't what I expected. The bags, of course, had been dropped in the middle of the kitchen floor, and the kids, all three of them, were squatting on the living room rug crooning over this cat.

I had this uncanny feeling that the cat knew my children by name and that it was familiar with my living room. I put down my three bags. "Candace, has this cat been in here before?"

Candace stood up and faced me defensively. She nodded slowly.

The scene looked too cozy. "This thing has been in our house … a lot?"

"Well … not that often. Aw, Mom, she's not that bad. She's a stray. She doesn't have a home, and everyone in the neighborhood loves her. Her name is Percy."

"Percy is a male's name."

"We all thought she was a male, but she had kittens."

I wanted that cat out. It looked as if it carried every flea in the neighborhood, not to mention every disease. I grabbed a broom and moved behind her to scare her through the open door, but Percy flashed behind the couch. When I poked at her, she streaked up the stairs. There was no way I could catch her.

Candace gave me a disgusted look, went upstairs, and called the cat gently. It came to her, and she carried it to the door.

"I don't want that cat in our house ever again," I said, matching Candace's look with one of my own.

Through the window, I watched as Percy scampered undaunted down our sidewalk to another friendly house. I couldn't help but stare. She was so odd looking. She must have been in an accident at one time, because she was slightly deformed and limped along like a strange-looking weasel, and her long black tail had a kink at the tip.

"She has got to be the ugliest cat I have ever seen," I said, and turned from the window in time to see the pain in Candace's eyes.

"Mom, don't say that. Percy is a wonderful cat. She's had it tough. Her kittens died. But she plays with us kids."

"You don't think she's ugly?"

"Once you get to know Percy, she doesn't look ugly anymore."

I turned back to the window. Now Percy was sitting on a white fence post.

"Mom, can we play with Percy? She really is good with kids. Syras loves her."

One could never be sure what kinds of diseases a stray cat might bring into the house, and I shuddered at the thought of that black hair against our pale yellow rug.

"She's been around for a year, and she's great, Mom," Candace pleaded. The other two kids stood on either side of her. "Please."

I turned back to the groceries. "As long as I don't know about it."

Candace smiled. It was all she wanted.

I didn't see Percy after that. I never found her in our house, and I never detected any black hairs on our rug. I assumed she had moved on to another neighborhood.

But the day Candace disappeared, the temperature dropped, and Percy was frantic to find a warm place. Since our door was opening and closing so often, she chose our house as her winter home. We had little choice in the matter because, without Candace, it was impossible to catch her.

I tried. I really tried.

Every time someone came to our door—and our door seemed to be revolving—she would jump up onto the steps, sneak through all the legs, and make one wild dash through the living room and up the stairs. She got so good at it that some of our guests didn't even notice her. Those who did had the strangest expressions as they felt that tiny thunder-cloud swirl between their legs and into the house.

"What was that?" someone would ask.

Usually there were more pressing things to consider than Percy, so we would just shrug our shoulders. Percy was a little hard to explain.

One evening, as we were visiting with friends, she came slinking down the stairs and stopped conspicuously in the hallway to survey the guests sitting in the living room, expertly assessing when they would be ready to say their good-byes and she would be able to make her escape. One of the guests gasped when he spotted her and said, "That has got to be the ugliest cat I have ever seen."

I instantly felt that same sense of frustration that I had when I first saw that cat. I had said those exact words not long ago. With her arched back, long legs, stubby body, bat-like face, and matted, scraggly fur, she was the ugliest cat I had ever seen too. Silhouetted against a moon, she would have been a perfect Halloween cat.

I felt the shame of having a cat in the house that represented everything ugly. Now that we were having all these guests coming and going in our house, the cat represented our poverty, our messiness, and our complete failure in everything. Her black hair was everywhere.

I began to obsess about Percy. I wanted that cat gone—and I tried to keep up with the black hair.

The impact of violence or betrayal of any magnitude will naturally rob us of the feeling that we are in control of our lives. And just as naturally, our egos will have problems with this. Ego likes control.

Ego is the sum total of who we are; everything we do, every move we make, every step we take, is connected to our ego. Without delving into the complex and contested theories of psychoanalysis typified by Sigmund Freud, I just want to define ego as synonymous with self. One of the purposes of ego is to protect us from harm. Whenever there is a threat, it is on alert and overly vigilant.

That is why when we feel wounded, every slight, every misunderstanding, every negative nuance, judgment, and feeling of disrespect is heightened and magnified. We are hypersensitive to every reaction to us. Our defensive ego begins to cycle, to fret, and to scheme ways of trying either to defend ourselves or to retaliate. We want to fight everything, distrust everyone, and do away with anything that is causing this enormous stress in our mind, body, heart, and spirit.

In this panicked state, we can lose sight of the broader pictures and obsess about the little things. Or we won't be able to concentrate on the details, we lose all sense of time, can't read, can't concentrate, can't absorb anything we deem meaningless.

For example, it was so easy at the end of day to obsess about the way the police were handling the investigation, how the community was reacting to our story, how our friends wouldn't get it right. We wanted to confront the justice system, our friends, our church, and our family because they were immediate and in our faces, rather than focus on the real source of the problem—the abduction of Candace.

Ego gives us a sense of control—a false sense that we can do something about the uncontrollable. In the end we will have to discern what we can control and what we can't control, and address what we can control.

Sitting on the edge of the mountain, the Nazarene sees a group of young men with their backs to him, watching the sea but still listening. The gentle teacher, knowing what they are planning, says to them:

> You have heard that it was said, "Eye for eye, and tooth for tooth." But I tell you, do not resist an evil person. If anyone slaps you on the right cheek, turn to them the other cheek also. And if anyone wants to sue you and take your shirt, hand over your coat as well. If anyone forces you to go one mile, go with them two miles. Give to the one who asks you, and do not turn away from the one who wants to borrow from you ... that you may be children of your Father in heaven.

In this teaching there are three radical statements. First, he says that a person should turn the other cheek when someone strikes him. Second, he says that his followers should give those who use them more than they are asking. Third, he says that a person conscripted by a Roman officer to carry a load for one mile should offer to go two miles.

Let's just address the first statement here. The slap described here is an insult rather than a physical assault with the intent of depriving an individual of life or health. But even so, the natural human tendency when insulted is to seek the emotional satisfaction of revenge. But according to this directive, petty insults and dishonors are not worthy of fighting. As victims, we are often dishonored by the little things people say to us. It is easy to dwell here, to take offense with the tiny slights rather than address the huge injustices that we encounter.

Odia had a friend over one evening. Cliff and I were sipping our after-dinner coffee when Odia's friend casually commented on the jokes about Candace circulating in the school. When we asked them what kind of jokes they were, both girls shot out of the house.

Later we asked Odia again. She stalled and bit her lip.

"How many jokes are there?"

"Two."

"Are they about us?"

"No."

"Are they about Candace?"

She looked away.

"Would they hurt Candace?"

She continued to look at the wall.

"Would they hurt us?"

She nodded.

"Do they hurt you?"

"Yes."

I would have loved to leave it at that. But just by her guarded response, I knew that whatever it was, it was too big of a burden for a little girl. She needed to share it with us to lighten the load.

"Does the joke make fun of Candace?"

Odia nodded.

"Please, Odia, tell us," I begged.

She took a deep breath. "It's a stupid joke. The joke is: What did the Derksens get for Christmas?"

We shrugged our shoulders and waited.

"Candy in a box."

I felt the edge of a cold stainless steel blade slit my heart—not so much for myself but for the young face in front of us putting up such a brave fight for control. She told us the other joke, and it was much the same. Odia looked shredded after she had told us.

I thought I would die from the pain. But I didn't. Murder was worse.

The Nazarene is saying the same thing, "Don't sweat the small stuff. We have bigger concerns." Or, "Choose carefully which hill you want to die on."

If we keep our focus on the bigger concerns in life, we can more easily overlook the little things like the car cutting us off. I had to let go of my need to control how I was being treated.

Our guest who had called Percy the ugliest cat was right. But I had to shake off the shame. It didn't take us too long to realize that Candace had been right. There was something special about Percy. She didn't like us adults any more than we liked her, but she loved children. Syras would follow her around the house, and she knew how to stay one short, chubby arm's length away from him, keeping him amused for hours. She made the children laugh; she made us smile. She was an ugly black angel—but an angel nonetheless. She was so much more than black hair. I asked Cliff if he would pick up kitty litter and some cat food on his way home from a search-committee meeting. She had become a welcome part of the fabric of our lives.

It really didn't matter what people would think.

_____

I had to let go of my ego, my need to defend myself, and I had to take the high road.

_____

Chapter 9

LETTING GO OF MY NARROW FAITH

> *Forgiveness is God's greatest gift.*
>
> —DAN BROWN

A t first I remember being so confident about God. I had no choice really—everything was out of control and we needed a higher power. But over the years, slowly, my resentment grew as it became more and more apparent that God wasn't about to fix anything we asked for. He hadn't helped us find Candace when it was critical. When her body was found, he didn't help us find the person responsible. When the lies and innuendoes were swirling, he didn't help us with any resolution of any kind. Nothing went our way. Nothing!

I just became very tired of facing the adverse wind of life. I became more disillusioned with God's ability to maneuver anything. He became a very distant God to me. He became more and more distant until I deemed God more or less worthless.

I thought perhaps he had lost interest in us and his grand flop of a creation. God was just good for heaven and those with a naive faith. When it came to the real issues, like good and evil or the complicated things like my life, he had left the building a long time ago.

I was also resentful because everyone else seemed to have ordinary lives. I had no idea why we had been picked out of the crowd like this to be put onstage in the cruelest way. For it to be so pointed, God must have had something to do with it.

Ordinarily I could deny these doubts and push them out of my mind and pretend everything was good, but there was one song that would not let me.

Every time the congregation would sing it, I would well up with volcanic emotions ready to burst and flood the entire sanctuary—or at least that is the way it felt. I hated the song—not only the words but the story behind it. And it seemed to haunt me.

> When peace, like a river, attendeth my way, When
> sorrows like sea billows roll;
> Whatever my lot, Thou has taught me to say, It is
> well, it is well, with my soul.

The song, penned by Horatio Spafford and composed by Philip Bliss, was written after several traumatic events in Spafford's life. The first was the death of his only son in 1871, shortly followed by the Great Chicago Fire, which ruined him financially. He had been a successful lawyer. Then in 1873, he had planned to travel to Europe with his family on the SS *Ville du Havre*, but sent the family ahead while he was delayed on business concerning zoning problems following the Great Chicago Fire. While crossing the Atlantic, the ship sank rapidly after a collision with a sailing ship, the *Loch Earn*, and all four of Spafford's daughters died. His wife Anna survived and sent him the now-famous telegram, "Saved alone." Shortly afterwards, as Spafford traveled to meet his grieving wife, he was inspired to write these words as his ship passed near where his daughters had died:

> It is well, with my soul,
> It is well, it is well, with my soul.

After ten years, I could no longer deny my growing cynicism. I couldn't play church anymore—so we went looking for a new kind of church. One that had no windows. One that was dark. One where the minister spoke often about the abyss.

We shouldn't be surprised if the criminal violation of society's moral code and social contract calls into question the order and control of the entire universe and the role of the Creator of that universe in all of this. There is an obvious disconnect that comes with a violation.

But anger toward God can result in a dreadful darkness. The dark night of the soul is a time in which we don't feel God's presence, we don't hear his voice, and it seems that God has left us on our own. It can be a depressing time—dry and distant from God. We feel the universe has targeted us, cursed us, is punishing us, or has failed us dreadfully.

I remember driving home from work one day worried about Odia. Now that she was a teenager, she was manifesting the usual teenage angst.

I still remember turning into the back lane of our house on Hazel Dell—everything was slushy and dirty. It all felt familiar. I was tired and feeling stretched from trying to be conscientious in my work while carrying quite a lot of volunteer work and still being the devoted mother.

What to do about Odia? My fallback position was always to pray—give it to God. But I didn't pray. I couldn't pray.

I was puzzled. I had no trouble praying for Candace's legacies or my work; why didn't I want to pray for Syras or Odia? Why not them? Then I realized I didn't want God to know I had other children.

I couldn't trust my other two children to a God who had let Candace die.

It is hard to remain pure after being violated. It is hard to resist aggressively acting out on one's frustrations. As Friedrich Nietzsche said, "And if you gaze long into the Abyss, the Abyss also gazes into you."

When we have experienced an injustice, as victims we almost immediately feel that we have been given permission to act in kind. We are entitled. We have seen an example of ugliness, and we are prone to copy. I met many victims in prisons.

Wounded, we are also tempted to give into pleasure to comfort ourselves. We are tempted to commit all kinds of adultery—emotional, spiritual, physical—and change loyalties. This attitude of resentment, this blaming anger toward God, doesn't hurt God; rather, it only results in us locking him out and not seeing him. Our perception of God determines how we see him. When this happens, we need to let go of our anger and resentment toward God.

My husband felt it helpful to start memorizing the Bible. He memorized huge portions of the book to find his way back to God. Waiting for God to show up differently for us.

Being more of a verbal processor, I would often find my way past my doubts and anger by having conversations with friends. When all else failed, late at night, I would open my Bible and read and read until some verse just jumped out, seemingly highlighted, and I knew it was God's voice speaking to me and encouraging me. It didn't matter what was highlighted; just the connection was comfort enough.

In dealing with doubt and anger toward God, we have two options, depending on our theology. If we truly think God is in control of everything that happens here on earth and is the one who actually allowed or intended the violation—in our case the murder of our child—we would have to forgive God and assume that God made a mistake. However, if we believe God didn't make a mistake, we might have to change our theology to recognize that, though God is the creator of the universe and controls the science of our world, he has given us freedom of choice, which means that he chooses not to control everything. Life happens. Evil exists.

In my resentment and blaming, I was forgetting that God was answering a prayer—a big, important, meaningful prayer that began at the end of summer when Candace had gone to babysit at a neighbor's house across the back alley.

Around nine at night she had called me. "I'm scared." This was highly unusual. Candace was always self-assured, daring, and fearless. So I went over and sat down on the rug beside her. We didn't say much at first. She seemed pensive. She beat me at a few video games, we munched on some peanuts, and then I finally broached the subject. "Why are you scared?"

"I had a nightmare." A teacher of hers had kept her in a well, a deep, dark well, wanting to kill her.

I questioned her at length to see if this dream of hers had any basis in reality; it clearly didn't. She didn't think so either. It had just frightened her, she said over and over.

Not understanding it, I chose an easy answer. "Candace, if you are afraid, pray that God will protect you—and then live. God will send his angels to protect you."

It seems like a simplistic answer in hindsight, but it was a ploy that I had used as a child. Back then I had memorized Psalm 34:7: "The angel of the Lord encampeth round about them that fear him, and delivereth them." And I had truly believed it, making me quite fearless growing up. If it worked for me, it might work for her.

I'll never forget how she looked at me with her big blue eyes and asked, "Mom, can you tell me, honestly, that if I pray to God to protect me, that nothing will ever hurt me again?"

So much for my old-fashioned, simplistic answers. My daughter had grown up.

I too had evolved in life to a place where the verse was no longer enough. I had asked the same question when we had encountered our first threat. Managing a store in a northern community, Cliff had been threatened often, and for an entire evening had been held at knifepoint, leaving us both feeling vulnerable and afraid.

Later, I met a relative who had come to terms with danger and threats to his life, and I asked him what had helped him. He told me of his belief that should his life be ended prematurely in a violent way, his God would then be responsible to make his death have more of an impact than his life. In his view, murder would add value to his life's impact rather than devalue it.

I told Candace the story. I told her that I believed that death is not the worst option. To live a life with no value, no meaning, no impact is far more tragic. Murder would double the impact of our lives. We needed to give our fear of murder to God, who would then be forced to settle it.

Oh, how glibly I spoke! Especially since we now lived in the safe community of Elmwood close to the heart of the city of Winnipeg. But it sounded like a great way to deal with an unreal threat.

She didn't answer me right away.

Finally I asked, "Are you okay, Candace?"

She looked up, and I saw that there were tears in her eyes. "Yes, Mom."

I knew something had happened inside of her. Something

had changed. She had accepted my hypothesis, and it had comforted her, just like it did for me. It was a wonderful hypothesis to guard against something that would never happen.

She said I could go home now; she would be alright. Only a few months later—November 30, 1984—she disappeared on her way home from school. Seven weeks later her body was found, hands and feet tied, left to die in the plunging temperatures of a Winnipeg winter. The police classified it as first-degree murder.

I remembered our talk.

Oh my God, what had I told her?

I had not only given her an untested hypothesis to comfort her, but I had also put out a challenge to the Almighty God. Did I have a right?

Of course, I couldn't just silently sit on the sideline and wait. As a mother, I swung into action, determined to make good out of her life, as I had promised.

Amazingly, her seemingly short life did have an immediate impact. A swimming pool was built and named after her at Camp Arnes. Child Find Manitoba became a beautiful, well-established organization that was founded in her name. All kinds of little stories found their way to us about how Candace's short life and her murder had made an impact.

In hindsight I know God answered the prayers of my heart. He just didn't do it my way.

---

*I had to let go of my narrow faith that was often
highly manipulative and trust the Creator again.*

Chapter 10

LETTING GO OF THE OLD ME

> *I had to clear up my messy life. By letting go*
> *of the debris and filth, I have come to a deeper,*
> *more soulful beauty and clarity like an oasis in*
> *the desert. From that place of clarity, a vision of*
> *what I could have, what I could do, who I could*
> *be has emerged if I allow my heart to become a*
> *place of compassion, acceptance and forgiveness.*
>
> —SHARON E. RAINEY

We weren't really in the mood for a party, but we thought we would attend one as our first attempt at attaining some kind of normalcy after Candace disappeared. But when we entered the room, everyone stopped talking.

Ordinarily, Cliff and I weren't people who changed the atmosphere in a room. We weren't showstoppers—nor did we want to be.

I was a typical middle child who had only one ambition, and that was to be a writer—preferably writing historical romances where no one got hurt. Cliff wanted to be a small-time preacher like his uncle, and an artist on the side—nothing big. And we were close to our dreams. Cliff was a program director at one of the largest camps in Manitoba, which took advantage of all his gifts: designing brochures one minute, miming and strumming the guitar the next, taking pictures constantly, and even preaching once in a while. I had just finished a two-year course in journalism. We were so optimistic about our future.

We tried to mingle and enjoy a night out, when someone said quite offhandedly, "I could have killed him ..."

It was just a wife talking about how surprised she was to be publically embarrassed by a gesture of flowers, yet with us standing there it took on a whole new meaning. Everyone stopped and looked at us. The woman turned three shades of red.

Then we knew—our presence, so laden with victimization and violence, was not conducive to a good party.

Often a crime, betrayal, or murder can affect our social status. If those around us see us as losers, we will lose our honor or prestige. If they blame us for what happened, we fall from grace. We are stigmatized and marginalized.

Renowned neuroscientist Michael Gazzaniga notes, "When you get up in the morning, you do not think about triangles and squares and these similes that psychologists have been using for the past 100 years. You think about status. You think about where you are in relation to your peers."

Apparently this is normal for crime victims. Eric Schlosser writes in his article in *Atlantic Monthly*, "The victim is a defeated soul, a loser in this contest of strength. Perhaps it is easier to identify with the murderer. To do otherwise means choosing the side of the powerless."

There are many consequences to being edged out. Our self-esteem, our identity, and especially our productivity is influenced by our status in society.

Society as a whole finds victimization very difficult to deal with. According to Lula Redmond, society believes that "those who are murdered have in some way led to their own death.... By these explanations, a protective shield is set up within the mind of the observer that the circumstances are such that the tragedy would never happen to them."

Some of it was understandable—people were reacting to the changes in us. Our values, our interests, and even our entertainment tastes were changing.

As Christmas day approached, people began to make special overtures to make sure we weren't alone on that day, except we were feeling more and more ill at ease with everyone's plans for us. We didn't feel like Christmas, and we didn't want to spoil anyone else's Christmas, so we decided to spend Christmas alone—without anyone knowing.

We tried to have a traditional Christmas Eve alone. It was dismal—intolerable.

So the next day, when it came time to eat our Christmas dinner, we hopped into the car to look for a place to eat. We had purposely not made any reservations, because we weren't celebrating; we were just eating out. We wanted a nice, ho hum family restaurant. But we had never been out on the streets on a holiday before, so we were surprised to find that all the family restaurants were closed. We decided that even McDonald's would do, but it was closed too.

To lighten the moment, Cliff said, "This is probably the most authentic Christmas we will ever have—just like Joseph and Mary looking for a place to settle and finding nothing open."

We eventually found a small, greasy-spoon cafe that was open. It seemed specially designed to let the bitter cold wind howl right through the front entrance and out the back. We fit right in with all the leftover people who obviously had no place to go. Without even talking to any of them, we seemed to know each one's story.

I'm sure their head cook was having his Christmas at home, because the food was the worst I've ever eaten. None of us could finish our plates.

Next we went to see *Pinocchio*, a Disney classic. It was a safe choice, we thought. But not far into the movie, we found ourselves watching a heartbroken Geppetto out looking for his lost, abducted son.

Cliff and I looked at each other over the kids' heads. In the dim light, barely able to see his eyes, I knew what he was thinking. *There is no escape. There is no relief, not even in a simple Walt Disney movie.* We couldn't go around it, under it, or over it.

We had fundamentally changed. Even our taste in movies would be forever changed.

It felt as if we would never fit in again.

The experience of violence or any kind of injustice reorders the sense of self. It devastates our identity. Our values, interests, lifestyle, attitudes, and habits can be so drastically altered that we almost become unrecognizable.

On the other hand, there are those who find a new identity in victimization that is conducive to their needs. They will quite easily adopt a new trauma identity for themselves—something more than just an event that happened in their life.

But for the most part, when something drastically changes our identity, whenever we find ourselves wondering "Who am I?" or "What are people thinking of me now?" we can lose confidence to move forward. We become traumatized in a different way.

It's not easy to find ourselves again.

Somehow we managed to survive in our jobs for the first ten years after Candace's death, but after that I wanted to change my identity completely. Surely by now people had forgotten our story, and I could just start fresh, doing anything I wanted to do. I wanted to get away from anything introspective.

I decided to go into real estate. I took the course, received my license, and found a wonderful partner.

Finally, it came time to actually show my first house all by myself. It was a little house in my area that an elderly couple was selling so they could move into an independent living community. This was their first step in downsizing.

I sensed their grief, their anguish, and their fears as we set up the parameters of that first show.

A promising client came through the door, a middle-aged man who asked all the right questions as we went around the first floor. When that was completed, we went into the basement. Somehow we all felt a little more vulnerable in the basement, which was unfinished for the most part.

That's when the man cleared his throat. "By the way," he looked directly at me, excluding the owners very deliberately in his body language and eyes, "I haven't come to buy a house."

From the corner of my eye, I could see the startled reaction of the owner of the house: instant anger. The man continued. "I've come to see you," he said, still holding my eyes with an astonishing fierceness.

I was confused. "Me?"

"Yes, my daughter was murdered."

Wrong place. Wrong time.

I glanced at the owners; their eyes were huge. "Who are you?" they asked.

The stranger told them that I wasn't a real estate agent, but I was a mother of a murdered child. In absolute frustration, I made an appointment with him to meet another time and ushered him out, trying to console the disappointed owners.

I resigned shortly thereafter. Yes, I was a real estate agent, and yes, I was also the mother of a murdered child. Both were part of my new identity. I realized, though, that I had tried to use my job to deny who I had become. I couldn't do both; they weren't compatible. I had to choose one.

I called the director of a victim/offender restorative justice program. He was in town—miraculous timing, he said. We met at Aalto's Cafe.

"If you had the position with us, what would you do?" he asked.

I hadn't even thought of that. I thought they would define my role—if they wanted me.

What an opportunity! I took a napkin and started to outline my dream for the position—taking it one step further than anything I had ever done.

"I will take this and see," he said, pocketing my scribbled proposal.

That was it. They called me soon after, and I went to work for them.

I became a social researcher of sorts, which incorporated all of my new identities. I was a parent of a murdered child, a writer, a journalist, a coach, a facilitator, and a perpetual student of a cutting-edge field: forgiveness.

I had to let go of the old me and make peace with my new identity. Some doors were closing to me; some were opening. And those doors that were opening for me were even better than the ones I would have chosen for myself.

Chapter 11

LETTING GO OF MY EXPECTATION THAT LIFE IS FAIR

*A single gentle rain makes the grass many
shades greener. So our prospects brighten on
the influx of better thoughts. We should be
blessed if we lived in the present always, and
took advantage of every accident that befell
us, like the grass which confesses the influence
of the slightest dew that falls on it; and did not
spend our time in atoning for the neglect of past
opportunities, which we call doing our duty.
We loiter in winter while it is already spring.*

—HENRY DAVID THOREAU, *WALDEN*

It was a cold evening, but that did not matter. We hadn't
seen each other for a few years, and we were just glad
to see each other again. A group of us parents of murdered
children were meeting in a dingy church basement. We had
tried to decorate it and provide good food, but there was no
denying the fact that our chosen setting was very humble
and not all that comfortable.

As we hobbled into the room, we simply burst out laughing. We looked terrible. Most of us had some kind of elastic bandages, some were on crutches, some had canes, some of us had put on a lot of weight. Life had not been kind to us, and it showed.

Shortly after that, I was asked to give a presentation at William Head, a prison institution forty-five minutes outside of Victoria on Canada's western shore, a beautiful point of land surrounded by the Strait of Juan de Fuca. This institution is known for its progressive and creative programs. The prisoners there exuded an air of confidence, enthusiasm, and, to some degree, comradery that I hadn't seen in the other institutions. These men were well looked after.

I immediately had a big case of "penal envy." I wanted to gather the group back home with their bandages, canes, and crutches and bring them here and take over the institution. We were the ones who needed a safe place with a guard at every corner. We would relish institutional food that we wouldn't have to make. We would love to be tucked away from the public glare and protected with huge walls around us. We would love the time to just stare at a TV monitor. We wouldn't care much what we slept on because we weren't sleeping anyway.

This isn't a criticism of our penitentiaries. I personally am proud of a country that looks after our institutions and inmates so well. It reflects a generous, loving culture that values everyone. But on the other hand, I ache for those who aren't looked after as well.

After a murder, it is known that if a house has been the crime scene, it will fall in value at the same time the family might need to move from the memories. This can result in a spiral of losses, failed marriages, loss of work, inability to func tion socially, and even a decline in health. After a betrayal, we might need to deal with severance packages, lawsuits, divorces, and investment losses. Often, injustices not only violate a relationship but also threaten a person's employment, sustainability, and ability to live independently, and usually bring financial hardships.

The hardest part of a crime is that the victims expect that the person responsible for the loss, the person breaking the law and stealing or murdering or whatever, would be the one to compensate, but usually they aren't able to. Often there is no hope of compensation. The person violating usually has nothing to give, or it is irreparable crime, such as ours. There is no fairness and no justice.

Turning these difficult circumstances around requires radical, frightening actions. To change employment, move to another province or state, or take time off is unsettling in an already chaotic and unsettled life. Nothing about this is fair. And yet sometimes the feelings around the injustices are more damaging than the actual event.

It was twenty-two years after Candace's murder. I was just about to call Cliff on his cell when I noticed his van pull up on the driveway. He came in breathing heavily, carrying two large bags—basically his transportable office for his janitorial business.

We were expecting a visit from the police force; four men were coming to tell us something. It was our first major visit from them since Candace's body had been found.

"Have to shower," he said, taking off his jacket and starting down the hallway to the bedroom. "I feel grimy."

"No time to shower." I followed him, picking up his bags and taking them to his office so they would be safely out of sight. "They are going to be here any minute. Put on something black."

"Why black?"

"No time to discuss it. Just wear something black."

He was already taking off his shirt when I walked into the bedroom. "Black, always black. What is it with you and black?" he grumbled. Something in his tone told me that this wasn't about me. He was as worried as I was.

"Confidence," I said. "It's all about confidence. And we need all the confidence we can muster for this visit."

He picked out black trousers and a charcoal shirt from his closet. I nodded my agreement. "I've made coffee for them," I said. "But I don't have any bottled water. I forgot to pick some up."

He smiled. "I forgot to pick up donuts," he said, chuckling. "I promised them donuts."

I winced. "No donut jokes. Please—no donut jokes."

A few moments later, there were three men at our door, tall and all dressed in black. I invited the officers into the living room, noticing that there were only three. I had been told there would be four. What did that mean?

I took their heavy leather jackets and hung them in the

closet. They took off their black shoes. I protested, but they did it anyway.

Five of us—all dressed in black—were sitting in my predominantly white living room. It would have been a striking picture.

Nothing they could have said would have eased the tension. I don't remember the conversation word for word, but it went something like this, starting with one of them leaning forward.

"We found him," he said. "We have found the man who murdered Candace."

We just sat there. Our minds were racing in a million directions. They were waiting for a response.

"Are you sure?" I said finally. Was this a ploy? I just couldn't believe them.

"Yes."

I looked at each one of them separately. They all nodded.

"Do we know him?"

"No, you don't," said the man who started the conversation.

"Are you sure we don't know him?"

He leaned slightly forward. "And I just want to let you know it isn't anyone known to your family."

The supervisor, who was sitting beside me, repeated, "It isn't anyone you know."

"No one we know," I said in disbelief.

They must have said it a dozen times in different ways.

"Aren't you relieved?"

We nodded. Our poor, traumatized minds could not

absorb it, even as I nodded. It was hard to erase twenty-two years of careful defense building in one second.

What a disappointment it must have been for them. Here they had done such splendid police work, and all we could do was sink into the past.

Then they told us that they would be picking him up in two to six weeks and that they had a team of twelve officers working on it. It was pending.

We talked about every detail, again and again. Once we were finally satisfied, they left. Could justice be a possibility after all this time?

What a relief. Cliff sank down onto the sofa. "I'm not going to jail," he said. He was sitting there, slumped, drained, and relieved.

I was surprised. "All these years you always thought you might land in jail?"

He nodded.

It had been twenty-two years. We hadn't even realized the weight of the cloud until it was lifting.

And I'm glad we hadn't focused on the cloud. We had been too busy working to keep a roof over our heads. Justice had come on its own time, and no amount of worrying, fretting, or focusing on it would have made it come sooner.

I had to let go of my expectation that life
is fair and that I would be compensated
for all my losses. I had to concentrate
on containing the spiraling losses.

Chapter 12

LETTING GO OF MY GUILT AND BLAME

When you forgive, you love. And when you love, God's light shines upon you.

—JON KRAKAUER

The first anniversary day of Candace's disappearance fell on a Saturday, and when we got up that morning, it had all the markings of being just an ordinary day. I wondered if by ignoring it, just not talking about it, we might not really notice it. But right from the beginning, even without any words, I could tell that a cloud had descended on us. Even the kids sensed it and seemed preoccupied.

By afternoon, I was desperate to escape from the heavy mood, and I tried to rouse Cliff into making some last-minute plans. Couldn't we at least go shopping?

Cliff had retreated to the basement to work on the computer, and he looked up from his swirl of papers, irritated. I suddenly knew that his absorption was his escape, and he was comfortable in it.

I prowled around the house a bit longer and then decided that maybe Cliff had the right idea. I needed to drown myself in work, hard work. The hardest work I could think of was washing walls.

I should have known it wouldn't work. I'm never in the best of moods when I'm housecleaning as it is; why would it be any different this day of all days? I could tell that instead of losing myself in the scrubbing, I was just becoming more and more irritated.

I stared at the hundreds and hundreds of little finger-prints. Did the kids touch the walls all the time? Were they blind? Did they find it impossible to walk down a hall or down the stairs without feeling where they were going?

As I worked my way down the stairwell, I glanced at my watch. It was getting closer and closer to four o'clock. I started to understand the importance of an anniversary. It is probably the closest to the original moment one ever gets.

Time seemed to stand still. Why was this moment so terrifying? What actually happened this time a year ago? Suddenly, I knew! This was not only the anniversary of the day that Candace disappeared; it was also the anniversary of my decision not to pick her up.

Fingerprints were on the wall above the bottom step, and I wondered how they had gotten there. Cliff and I never touched that section of wall, and Odia and Syras were too small. Only Candace, like every teen I knew, would hang onto the doorjamb and swing herself out over the main floor. I looked closer. They were her size.

Immobilized, I sat on the stairs looking up at them. I couldn't wash off Candace's fingerprints. So little of her was left. How could I remove one more evidence of her life?

Without looking at my watch, I knew what time it was. It was five minutes after four. The moment was heavy with expectation, as if Candace might call any minute and I would be able to get into the car and pick her up and save all of us from going through the year of pain. We would have Candace again.

Suddenly the expectations turned into an accusation. Why hadn't I picked her up? This time there was no answer.

What kind of mother would allow her daughter to walk home in the cold at such a vulnerable time? Why hadn't I foreseen what was going to happen? There had been a number of other times when I had sensed that my children were in danger. I had found them perched precariously on top of the stairs or in the kitchen with a knife, but I had always been there to prevent the accident. This time, when the danger had been the most hostile, I had been preoccupied with finishing a writing project.

Why hadn't we been able to convince the police to get the dogs out when the scent was still fresh? We had done nothing! While she froze to death in a shed, we had been sitting in a warm house just waiting for her to die. It was all my fault. I could have prevented all of it from happening. She had died, and I had the audacity to survive and go on living.

The fingerprints seemed to grow larger.

I had no defense. The hideous voices were totally irrational, but guilt is irrational. It is a feeling that rarely responds to rational thinking. No matter how hard I tried to reason with it, I still felt guilty. I needed to deal with this feeling on a feeling level.

Blinking away tears, I stood up. The fingerprints needed to be removed. I wondered if it would be possible to remove them. I dampened my cloth and washed them away. There was a clean, white wall underneath. The whole house suddenly seemed sparkling clean.

With each stroke of washing the wall, I was washing away some of my guilt and self-blame. I had to let go of it. I had to forgive myself, which meant admitting my feelings of guilt and feeling the pain of my regrets. It wasn't only the fact that I hadn't picked her up that was the source of my guilt; I was also remembering all the times when I hadn't been the perfect mother.

After a betrayal or violence, the first instinct is to identify the primary cause of the harm. Who did it? We want to lay blame or we feel guilty.

The problem is that rather than identifying the person who actually did the crime, we will find a scapegoat—someone vulnerable, someone already flawed, or someone whom we might not want in our lives.

Chronic blaming can be a form of emotional abuse. Dr. Tom Jordan asserts that being blamed for an act that you did not actually commit is like taking a verbal beating. Someone subjected to a regular diet of blame may start believing that they are responsible for things that were beyond their control or with which they had nothing to do. Dr. Jordan reports that being a victim of a loved one's blame leads to self-blame and feelings of guilt. Thus, a subtle transition occurs, moving from the blamer's thoughts of *blaming you for the things that happen to me* to the thoughts of *blaming me for the things that happen to you.*

Down the road, the guilty feelings inevitably result in poor self-esteem and destroy relationships

I remember a case where a child was run over by a car, and the wife blamed the husband because he had been a few minutes late. She falsely reasoned that if he had been on time, none of it would have happened. It nearly destroyed their marriage.

Nothing is more detrimental to a relationship than false accusation. We need to think carefully about whom we blame or what we feel guilty for.

Sitting on the edge of the mountain, the Nazarene scans the crowd below him. He sees some older women—their faces creased—sitting together, whispering. He glances at them, holds them with his eyes. "Do not judge, or you too will be judged. For in the same way you judge others, you will be judged, and with the measure you use, it will be measured to you."

Here the word *judge* means distinguishing between something positive or negative. It means to separate. It assumes an intelligent comparison.

But, so often, intelligent comparisons aren't what we do. There is a big difference between the judge in a courtroom and our own inner judge. The judge in a courtroom hears all sides, considers the evidence, and then makes a fair judgment. Our own inner judge wants to quickly settle the issues, which often means blaming someone without always doing the research.

Often, in our need to vindicate ourselves, we will quickly point our finger at someone else, not realizing that every time we do that our own conscience will be tampered with and our sense of right and wrong will be compromised. The blame we issue then becomes our guilt. In the case of murder, blaming someone can have dire consequences. Many have been falsely accused.

Four months after Candace's death, Cliff was asked to come to the police station and take a polygraph test. The police said that they would like to test me later as well. By then we were familiar with a polygraph test. We had seen an extensive documentary on television about it, and since the investigation we had read about it. We knew that it would be a risk, and we discussed it as such. But the weight of our discussion was not on the risk of it but on how it might help the case.

Right from the beginning, we had been frustrated by the way the investigation had always centered on us. It was now April, five months after the fact, and they were still watching us. This request was just another sign of that. Maybe, just maybe, if Cliff took the test, they would finally look somewhere else.

Even though we knew the polygraph would not hold up as evidence in court and probably didn't have much credibility with the majority of people, we knew the police put a lot of stock in it. It spoke their language. Christine Jessop's parents from Queenston, Ontario, had said the same thing. When Christine's father had been accused of killing his daughter, he had taken the polygraph to convince the police. They had said it had worked.

We knew the risks, but I think at that stage we would have done anything—even sat in jail—to help clean up the case.

Two hours after Cliff left for the station, the possible implications hit me full force. If Cliff, for some strange reason, failed the test or the machine miscued, he wouldn't be coming home. He would be arrested for suspicion of murder! I was never so relieved as when Cliff walked through the door later that afternoon. He was shaken by the ordeal—but vindicated.

I had to let go of my guilt and blame.

Chapter 13

LETTING GO OF MY NEED TO KNOW

If truth doesn't set you free, generosity of spirit will.

—KATERINA STOYKOVA KLEMER

At the hospital, we pushed the big doors open. The assistant to the medical examiner slipped her arm around me, and we were taken into a private lounge and introduced to an officer from the homicide department.

"She doesn't look pretty," they said, starting to prepare us. "The blotches on her skin are from the cold. They aren't bruises." They gave us two Polaroid pictures, and my fingers trembled as I took them. It was Candace.

They were right; it wasn't a pretty picture. The horror of facing her own death was etched into Candace's face.

"I'm sorry," the medical examiner continued gently, "but we thought showing pictures would help to prepare you."

I wanted to tell her how grateful we were that they were being so considerate, but the tears wouldn't stop. They then briefed us on the details. They told us the body would be allowed to thaw, and that even though she might have died on the evening she disappeared, her death certificate would record January 17, 1985 as the date of her death.

We nodded mechanically.

They took us down an endless corridor and into a little white room. A tiny figure lay draped with a white sheet on what appeared to be an operating table.

This couldn't be Candace. In real life Candace was so much bigger. This was just a little corpse. But I forced myself to look closer. Yes, it *was* Candace. Candace minus her personality was so small, so terribly small, just a shell. Frozen so stiff, she looked like a dusty mannequin, and I drew back in horror. I didn't feel any attachment to what lay there. It was a grotesque duplication of something that resembled Candace's body, but it wasn't Candace.

They asked us if she looked the same as the day she disappeared. Was her hair the same? Her clothes? They wanted to determine how long she had been in the shack.

Yes, the clothes were the same; her hair was the same. Everything, as far as we could determine, verified that she had died that first night.

All of a sudden, I wanted to know everything that had happened from the time she had last talked to me until this moment, seven weeks later.

This was my child.

This was my responsibility. Who had done this? And why? It was more than a wish; it was a compulsion.

Years later, when asked to join a discussion on the roots of spiritual restorative justice at a very prestigious conference of well-known theologians, I remembered this moment.

Quite early on in the conference, they turned to me. "What do victims need?" they asked.

I remembered Candace motionless on the gurney. "They need the truth," I said.

One of the first things that disappears in the face of an injustice is the truth. Yet in order to make sense of the injustice or the crime, to restructure our lives and to build preventive safeguards, victims have a strong need to know what happened and why.

It is the quest of each court process to tell the truth, the whole truth, and nothing but the truth. It implies accuracy and honesty regarding real things, events, and facts. Sadly now, even in a court of law, placing one's hand on the Bible and declaring, "I swear by Almighty God to tell the truth, the whole truth, and nothing but the truth, so help me God," is no longer a guarantee that the truth will be heard. Victims learn this very quickly.

Around noon, the Nazarene smiles as he notices the busy mothers start giving their children lunch. He could tell that they were worried—that they were fretting about their physical needs, as every mother does when she wants to make sure her children are well cared for and safe.

But then he says, "Therefore I tell you, do not worry about your life, what you will eat or drink; or about your body, what you will wear. Is not life more than food, and the body more than clothes? ... Therefore do not worry about tomorrow, for tomorrow will worry about itself. Each day has enough trouble of its own."

Notice the emphasis on the word *worry*. It isn't the lack of resources or opportunities that is the problem—it is the worry that cripples us. We fret. We stress. We have anxiety attacks.

Worry occurs when we assume responsibility for things that are outside our control. Granted, the worry is more pronounced when we have just experienced something traumatic. We want answers and worry about what will happen if we don't get them. It takes great skill to disassociate from the past trauma and move into the present. When we have experienced loss, failure, or death, we are under no illusions that it can't happen. We know the reality of it.

Yet worry is useless. It gets us nowhere. This moment is the only moment that is real. The Nazarene is saying that if you focus on a counterintuitive lifestyle, then there will be enough for the day. And since we can only live one day at a time, we will always have enough.

But the need for truth is so strong. This was never so apparent as during the trial that happened twenty-six years after the murder of our daughter.

As victims, we just wanted the truth. I just wanted to know the story of what had happened, which was difficult as we listened to the testimony of the witnesses at the trial. We were finally hearing fragments of the truth twenty-six years later. I hung onto every word the medical examiner said as he described how the dirt on the tip of Candace's nose and also in the nostrils and slightly on the chin as well suggested that she was lying face down in the dirt. "And more importantly, as you see the legs there, the dirt on the legs, this suggests to me that she was lying face down at some time," he said, pointing to pictures I wasn't allowed to see.

Apparently, she had been found lying down on her face, and yet her lungs were clear of dust—she had not inhaled any of the dust.

The Crown, then looking at the photographs, continued. "Now in both photographs 20 and 21, I can see what appear to be red patches or splotches on the legs of the deceased. Looks almost like a sunburn. Can you tell us what that is please?" he asked the medical examiner.

"That is what we call lividity." He spelled it out, "L-I-V-I-D-I-T-Y, lividity, which is the passive settling of the blood shortly after death. It settles by gravity. It goes down. And so this means, together with other findings, that she was lying, at some point, face down, and that there's lividity. It's quite delineated, so that's passive blood. That's not an injury, just a postmortem change."

Even though we were listening intently during the court testimonies, we couldn't really put all the pieces together or connect the dots till later.

I decided to study the transcripts when we were back at home.

Face down but not touching the ground.

It meant that Candace, who had been hogtied, could have also been strung up and left to die hanging from the rafters. And then later, perhaps even a few days later, cut down and laid on her side, where she lay untouched until she was found seven weeks later.

I could feel my stomach knot. I got up from my desk and started wandering around the house, feeling confined.

Compelled, I went back to my desk. I needed to know!

Was it him? Was there concrete evidence that would convince me?

The words kept spinning as I reviewed it all and questioned it all again. Black hair, tawny hair, 1.2 mm, 5 inches, Ogilvie and Zacharias, the words kept tumbling around.

The truth that I had been so desperate for was now within reach.

The man on trial had actually said it. He had said that he "definitely" dyed his hair on a Wednesday, which was approximately two days before Candace was abducted on November 30, 1984.

Even though the pieces of information were scattered over the two-thousand-page transcript, I pieced it together. The person in the shed, the one with the unusual bleached hair who took Candace, showed a 1.2 mm root of hair. I didn't even need a calculator this time to know that 1.2 mm is two days and a bit!

It fit. Candace was taken on November 30. Two days before that was Wednesday, November 28.

"Definitely."

There it was! I went over it again and again. It was as good as a confession.

Seven hairs do tell the story. Four scalp hairs artificially altered—not for vanity's sake but to elude the police—are evidence.

He colored his hair to hide. Yet it was his hair that exposed him. Finally, I had my own personal, incontrovertible truth.

I waited for my rage. In the past, each time I moved toward certainty, I would have to face the reality again. But this time the rage didn't come. There was anger—a justifiable anger—but there was also something more. There was gratitude.

I had moved from a place of no reasonable doubt to certainty. I was finally convinced that the man on trial was guilty. It all fit together. The jury and the judge who had all the pieces had come to the right decision.

I was filled with gratitude, enormously grateful that I lived long enough to see this day—to see the end to my question. I was grateful to all those who played a role in finding Candace and investigating the case over the years. We had learned to live without answers. Now the answers were a pure gift.

Having wanted this information for thirty years, I understood the importance of it. I treasure it. But is it enough? Is this the final truth?

No—I don't think so. We will never stop learning. Life is all about the pursuit of truth, which will eventually set us free.

Even about this case. It is going to be retried again, which will probably raise even more questions. The learning will go on and on and on.

---

*I had to let go of my need to know
everything before I moved ahead; I had
to learn to function in the mystery.*

LETTING GO OF MY RAGE

Forgiveness is the key that unlocks the door of resentment and the handcuffs of hatred. It is a power that breaks the chains of bitterness and the shackles of selfishness.

—CORRIE TEN BOOM

I had a friend who came to visit me shortly after we had found Candace's body. She was a wonderful, no-nonsense kind of woman, a woman of integrity who demanded integrity from those around her.

We were having tea in our living room, and the sun was streaming in through the window.

Her first questions were about how we were doing. She affirmed that her impression of us was that we were forgiving—and doing it well.

But her next question caught me off guard. "If you could let yourself go, what would satisfy justice for you? Would it be execution?"

I had never allowed myself the question. I didn't think I was ready to face the complexity of it. But I felt safe with her, and her question was an interesting one. Perhaps it was time to think about it. I purposely loosened my controls and explored my inner feelings, my emotions. My friend waited in silence as I fell into deep thought.

"No," I finally answered, half to her and half to myself. "No, it wouldn't be enough. Execution, capital punishment, wouldn't completely satisfy me emotionally. If the offender were executed, he would be dying for something he did—he would deserve it.

"Candace was innocent. She died for no reason, for no fault of her own. She died young, in her prime, full of potential, full of anticipation, full of dreams, full of immediate plans of a good weekend. She would have contributed so much to our lives. Just to execute the offender would mean that he was being punished for what he had done. It would be removing a liability to society, a hopeless case. There's no equity in that."

I was shocked at my own answer. But I continued, "His death, one death, wouldn't satisfy me." I went deeper into myself, groping for the feeling of equity. "Ten child murderers would have to die." I paused, still groping for the satisfaction of justice. It was almost as if another voice answered for me. "And I would have to pull the trigger myself."

Oh, the feeling was wonderful! In my mind's eye I saw ten hooded figures lined up against a brick wall. There was a gun in my hand, and immediately I took advantage of the moment and aimed and pulled the trigger ten times. The feeling was delicious. They deserved to die. The figures fell one by one.

If I had been able to preserve my reverie of that moment, I'd now be in favor of the death penalty. It felt good. It felt so right. I understood the depth of my pain and the depth of my rage.

As the camera of my imagination continued to roll, I saw the hoods fall loose and expose ten faces vulnerable in death. I saw the blood and the desecration. I looked up and saw their families mourning the loss of their sons. And being so close to my own grief, I felt their loss as keenly as I felt my own. And worse yet—when I thought of it—was the possibility that one man might not have a family, might not have love in his life, and I would have snuffed out this last opportunity.

Then I met a psychologist who came up after one of my talks and said he had never felt the rage that I was describing. I was impressed! Wow—perhaps it was possible to be so evolved that one did not feel such gut-wrenching anger. But his daughter, who was standing next to him, looked at him in complete surprise. "You aren't angry?" she asked. I saw the disbelief in her eyes, then I saw him through her eyes: the tight jaw, that little throb …

We rarely know the depth of rage in our hearts. We have to ask those around us if we are angry. Our children and friends know.

The natural feelings of anger can take on unusual proportions after an injustice of this magnitude. When this explosive anger is directed toward society or other people, it becomes dangerous, uncontrollable, something we call rage. Rage is a pure, raw, and primitive emotion in the form of anger as a response to violence, betrayal, rejection, or bullying. Rage is a dramatic attempt to get back at the person who injured us.

Anger is a completely normal, usually healthy, human

emotion. "Anger can serve a number of useful, even vital, functions…. If judiciously exercised, it can enable a person to … compete for rank and position, strengthen bargaining positions, ensure that contracts and promises are fulfilled, and even inspire desirable feelings such as respect and sympathy." We know that Florence Nightingale was known for her anger against inadequate hospital care, which gave her the strength to battle the status quo and change medical care.

But when it gets out of control and turns destructive, anger can lead to problems—at work, in our personal relationships, and in the overall quality of our lives. And it can make us feel as though we're at the mercy of an unpredictable and powerful emotion. The average person feels some degree of anger or frustration ten to fourteen times a day.

Unresolved, smoldering anger can lodge itself in us but remain undetected for a long time and become a motivating force to make sure someone pays for the wrong that was done to us.

There are some healthy ways to get out of our angry state. Research shows that humor is a wonderful tension reliever. But sometimes the only way to deal with it is to change your environment. Leave. Count to ten. We need a safe place to process our anger and let any destructive emotion subside.

Midday, as it is getting hot, the Nazarene wipes his brow. He sees their hearts. "You have heard that it was said to the people long ago, 'You shall not murder; and anyone who murders will be subject to judgment.' But I tell you that anyone who is angry with a brother or sister will be subject to judgment."

Here in his Sermon on the Mount, the Teacher is saying that not only is murder wrong, but the emotions of wanting to kill that lead up to murder are as serious as the act itself. He is not only saying don't act it out, but he is drawing attention to the dangers of even fantasizing about murder.

After I admitted that I wanted to shoot ten people who had murdered children, I went back to our support-group members and asked them if they had felt the same things. Did they harbor revenge fantasies? I was surprised by what I heard. The revenge fantasies were powerful—and it felt as if they could become real at any moment.

The Nazarene teaches us that anger fantasies and murder are indistinguishable. If each person took responsibility for dealing with his or her anger and hatred internally, it could eventually eliminate the need for the police and the courts by stopping violence at its source.

As Lewis Smedes has said, "Hate can be fatal when we let it grow to enormous size inside of us. The best people can get their bellies full of it. And it is just as real whether it involves a nasty little scene between friends or a question of international immorality."

It is always hard to recognize when I've become angry. But when I do, I know it is a futile, puffed-up energy. I saw that as I talked to my friend. At the bottom of my heart, my murderous thoughts could, if left unattended, rise to the surface—and if I exploded, I would be the murderer. I would become everything I hated.

I was all alone. I remember stopping at the café at the bottom of the hill to quiet myself. It was a terrifying moment.
As I drove up, I had a chance to concentrate on the imposing
edifice of the castle-like penitentiary, its Tyndall stone his-
toric and intimidating.

It was thirteen years after Candace had been found
murdered that I responded to an invitation to visit a prison
institution. After passing through security, I was ushered
into the Lifer's lounge that was painted mellow beige. There
were about five huge fish tanks around the room.

For the first hour, the inmates described their organization, Lifeline, especially the peer support-group aspect of it.

First of all, they said that a life sentence meant life. That
even though they could apply for parole, not all of them
did. They would never get out on the street without being
monitored and on parole.

When I started to feel more comfortable, they asked me
about the needs of victims. What did I want? I said I just
wanted to feel safe to live my own life.

Then it was time for me to ask the questions I needed
answered. The agreement was that they would answer
anything.

The first question I asked was what crime landed each
of them in prison. We went around the circle. I noticed that
every race was represented.

There was a young man who had killed his common-law

wife. He said that he came from a family and lifestyle of violence. He was a slight man who thought he needed a gun to defend himself; he had never expected to use it.

There was a fair-haired man, about twenty five. He said that when his companion abused and hurt his child, he flew into such a rage that he killed her. He didn't know why, but in therapy he realized that he had been abused as a child, and he was really killing the person who had abused him. He couldn't make it in the outside world anymore, so when he was released he deliberately drank so he could go back to his comfort zone. He talked a lot about being institutionalized.

A young, handsome man killed his wife because she was making out with his friend—jealousy.

An intelligent man in the corner said he had experienced a mental meltdown when his thirteen-year marriage broke up. There had been numerous losses, too many. He couldn't remember the killing.

A younger man said he had been a street kid and involved in drug rings. When someone called him a goon, his honor had been at stake, and he killed the man. His second killing was in keeping with the first. He didn't know that he had options. He didn't know that he could walk away from an insult or a threat.

A balding army type said that he had killed his best friend when he was challenged to a fight over a woman. When his friend drew a weapon, the man used his army skills to fight and kill his friend.

One man said that he was simply too proud to commit suicide, so he hurt and killed others instead. He was in prison because of drug-related killings. He was the first to tell me that he couldn't look at himself in the mirror for six months after the murders because the remorse had been so real.

Another man said that he came from a strong patriarchal family where everyone just assumed that you could be strong, keep the family happy, and never show anger. But he blew up and killed his wife.

I asked them how much time they were sentenced to and how much time they had done. Then I asked them how they felt now that they had been charged and sentenced for murder. They said they were humiliated and ashamed.

I asked them what their explanation for murdering was, and they gave that answer solemnly and without rationalization. Anger led each one of them to kill. They were all very careful to say that it wasn't an excuse for what they had done. None of them looked like killers.

I wish I could remember more. I wish I could remember every word that was spoken. All I know is that at the end of the afternoon, I didn't want to kill them. I understood them and valued very much what they had given me.

There were exactly ten men in that room.

I had to let go of my rage and redirect
my energy into battling for good.

Chapter 15

LETTING GO OF MY OBSESSION WITH THE OFFENDER

> *Forgiveness has nothing to do with absolving a criminal of his crime. It has everything to do with relieving oneself of the burden of being a victim—letting go of the pain and transforming oneself from victim to survivor.*
>
> —C. R. STRAHAN

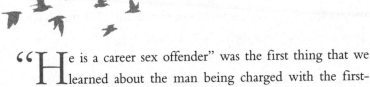

"He is a career sex offender" was the first thing that we learned about the man being charged with the first-degree murder of our daughter. "He blames his hatred of women on his mother and sister and has a twenty-year resume of crime to show for his anger."

We just sat there for a moment, stunned, trying to absorb it and feeling numb. We were scheduled to meet at the Public Safety Building downtown for the press conference that would break the news to the rest of the city.

As we parked the car, I noticed that as we got out my foot was hurting, the pain quite severe. I wondered if I could walk all the way to the building but then decided I didn't have time to think about it right then. I decided to ignore it

When we entered the Public Safety Building, we met the chief of police and then were ushered into the press room. I was in a bit of a daze that entire day. But I remember that my ankle was really aching for some inexplicable reason. It had never hurt before, and I was having trouble focusing.

The Winnipeg police had entitled the media release, "Project Angel Leads to Arrest in 1984 Candace Derksen Homicide." The statement covered the entire story. When the police chief had completed his statement, Cliff read our statement. "We are grateful for this moment," he read. "Of course, with this comes a renewed sense of sadness that has never left, and never will, at the loss of our daughter. It also reminds us of the horrors of her passing." What should have been a happy moment was awash with the haunting memories of when it all began.

Then the press conference was thrown open to entertain questions from the reporters. The first round of questions was directed to the police, to Cliff, and then one directed to me.

"Have you forgiven?" one of the reporters asked.

The idea of *forgiveness* looked very different now that we knew that there was an identified person. For one thing, forgiving someone presumes guilt, and we didn't know if he was guilty. Officially he was accused but would remain innocent until proven guilty. Besides, with our history of Cliff being falsely accused in the public arena, we didn't want to presume the man was guilty before we knew the facts.

I had read somewhere that there are differences in our reactions to certain crimes. There is of course the horror of murder, the ultimate crime of taking someone's life. But there is also another horror that is almost equal, and that is sexual assault. I was now facing both. I didn't know—I hadn't had any time to process.

I wanted to avoid the question. I hesitated.

As before, the next day some of the headlines picked up on the forgiveness theme just as they had so long ago. The first line of one news article read, "Wilma Derksen admits that she overestimated her emotional abilities when she pledged forgiveness." A *Winnipeg Free Press* article was entitled "Girl's Parents Unsure about Forgiving Killer."

That wasn't entirely true. I would forgive, I wanted to forgive, and I believe forgiveness is the only way. But in order to truly forgive, there needs to be integrity, and for the first time we were facing a new issue.

So while I was trying to figure this out, my ankle was still bothering me. I was in real pain, desperate pain. I'm not used to my body protesting so much. The shooting pain up my leg was telling me that I was not letting go.

Finally, three nights later and still in pain, I decided to open my Bible. The words from the Sermon on the Mount jumped out at me. "But I tell you, love your enemies and pray for those who persecute you ..."

I dissolved into tears and cried and cried as if my heart was breaking all over.

Then I got up from my desk. I printed out the pictures of the man who had murdered our daughter. I placed two pictures at eye level on my bookshelf.

I prayed for him that night.

The next morning, my ankle felt different. It was sore, but I didn't feel the sharp pains. The day after, I was healed.

Even though for many years we didn't know who had murdered our daughter, there seemed to be this kind of invisible push/pull experience with the unknown perpetrator.

I sometimes considered him a member of our extended family. On my speaking tours, when I met friends we hadn't seen for a while, they inevitably would ask how Cliff was doing. I usually answered that we were still married. We would laugh about that, knowing how the odds were stacked against us. Then they asked about Odia and Syras. Finally they would ask about the person who killed Candace. Had he been found? Were there any clues? Now they asked how the trial process was going and whether he had been found guilty or not.

Some have described this feeling as being tied to one end of a long rope, with the offender on the other end, for a long game of tug-of-war. How does one resolve this delicate, traumatic, and complicated relationship?

There is a strong belief that all conflicted relationships need to be resolved. We have been taught that forgiveness means to restore a bond of love and communion when there has been a rupture. And ordinarily, when there are two people with the same spirit, the same goals, and the same ethics having a dispute, it is easier to come to a resolution.

It is much different if there are moral issues at stake.

Lewis B. Smedes says it well in his book, *The Art of Forgiving*:

> Let it be shouted once more, from the roof this time: Forgiving a person does not mean that we tolerate what that person is doing to hurt us. Forgiving does not turn us into mush.
>
> Forgive a wife-slammer if you can, but you don't have to live with him. Forgive a husband who is abusing your children, if you can, but only after you kick him out of the house. And if you can't—get help. It is available.... In the meantime, don't let him near the kids, and don't let anyone tell you that if you forgive him it means you have to stay with him.

He also writes:

> I repeat these three fundamental points because when people ask how often they should forgive, what they usually want to know is how much abuse they need to put up with. They are not really talking about forgiving. They are asking about tolerating. And they need to understand that forgiving and tolerating are different species as different as cantaloupe and basketballs....
>
> What sorts of things should we not tolerate? Any

morally healthy person knows them when she experiences them, but it can't hurt to mention a few. Cheating on a partner is intolerable. So is abusing a child. Or lying to a friend. Forcing sex on a person who does not want it is intolerable. So is racism. Such things are intolerable under all conditions, in all cultures, in all times."

Forgiveness needs to be moral. It needs to have standards. It needs to distinguish right from wrong and uphold the right.

In the end, we are only responsible for our end of this victim-offender trauma bond. We can only control the end we are holding.

Squinting against the sun, the man from Nazareth sees two men glaring at each other from opposite sides of the crowd. "You have heard that it was said, 'Love your neighbor and hate your enemy.' But I tell you, love your enemies and pray for those who persecute you, that you may be children of your Father in heaven."

An enemy can be defined as anyone who doesn't love you, or someone who opposes you or is hostile toward you—an adversary.

This is perhaps the most controversial, misunderstood, and difficult part of the entire Sermon on the Mount. We are not to just force a smile and mind our own business when we are hated and mistreated. We are to actively do good toward our attackers. Agapaō is a rare word in Koine Greek. It was developed almost exclusively in Christian literature to refer to the kind of love that doesn't serve itself but extends itself for the sake of another.

The Nazarene must have spoken this part of the message more than once, using very strong action words in these verses: love your enemies, do good to those who hate you, speak well of them, and intercede for them.

Another word for love in this context is to embrace your enemy.

Loving our enemy doesn't mean becoming complicit with their actions or becoming culpable. It doesn't mean we enable, empower, or encourage wrongdoing. Our love is moral and remains uncompromised in its standards—but it is love nonetheless, love for those who make our lives unbearable.

I have to admit that I am always convicted when I read these words. I would like to water them down—say it isn't so—but I can't. The Nazarene's words are revolutionary.

Prayer for our enemies is one of the deepest forms of love, because it means that we have to really want something good to happen to them. Prayer is interceding on their behalf.

The first day of the preliminary hearing, we woke up to the rumblings of a summer thunderstorm as fierce as anyone could imagine. Flashes of lightning and cracks of thunder startled us over and over again. It was an eerie summer version of the storm that had come on the day we had buried Candace.

A few weeks prior, my sister and her husband had called to say they were preparing to drive to Winnipeg in their camper van to join us for the preliminary hearing.

A preliminary hearing had been described to me as a kind of dress rehearsal for the real trial. It was held in a small room, no bigger than a school classroom, in the new part of the Law Courts Building. The neutral beige room was furnished in the same way as all the courtrooms. The judge's desk was elevated in front, the box for the accused was to the right of it. The twenty chairs upholstered in dark fuchsia that composed the visitors' gallery were against the back wall. I decided to sit in the first row.

No sooner were we seated when the side door opened and the accused entered in shackles. *It is the one moment I've always dreaded. Am I meeting him? Is this the meeting I've anticipated?*

Our eyes met for a second. I had heard of the "glare moment" often shared between victim and offender on first sight. I didn't want to be caught in it. I didn't want to engage. I dropped my eyes to the beige rug and noticed that it was quite stained and worn.

Later, I learned that he had locked eyes with my sister and had refused to look down. She had been surprised at his obvious hostility. When I questioned my sister about the stare, she shuddered.

"Who won?" I asked, fully expecting her to win. She always won.

"He did," she said.

I was surprised. He didn't look threatening. I was also surprised at his general appearance. At home, I had two pictures of him that we had printed off the Internet; one was of him when he was younger with long, stringy hair—the proverbial "bad boy" image—the other as a middle-aged man, balding, with glasses and a moustache.

In the box he looked like neither one. He looked ill.

I was surprised by my calmness and thought it was all manageable—until the introduction of the exhibits. They brought in Candace's clothes as evidence—the clothes she had been wearing when she disappeared twenty-five years ago. My heart stalled. I could feel myself begin to perspire.

The police officer began to describe the evidence. "The deceased was wearing a high-school type jacket," he began. "It was a blue body with red burgundy-colored sleeves and wool cuffs. The deceased was also wearing blue jeans with ... and on her feet there were white socks." Someone brought in more plastic bags of evidence containing her jacket and her jeans. It felt as if she had walked into the room.

I was filled with unspeakable grief and longing for those days when we were so young and lighthearted, all of us, so filled with hope. Massive spasms of grief rocked the room. I began to shake. I felt I was losing control. Yet I couldn't let them see me cry. I had to be still, perfectly still.

And then I looked up. I looked up straight into Grant's eyes, fastened on me.

In naked grief, I stared into his eyes, the eyes of the man charged with the murder of my daughter.

I felt completely vulnerable, with no armor available. It seemed he had access to the inner torture of my soul, and I was defenseless. The power of the look felt like a violation, like an intrusion.

Nothing was said. No nodding. Not a flinch. But something passed between us. Something important.

I dropped my end of the rope. The tug-of-war was over.

I had to let go of my obsession with the offender
and my need for him to take responsibility
for what he had done to our family.

LETTING GO OF MY JUSTICE FANTASY

I have always found that mercy bears richer fruits than strict justice.

—ABRAHAM LINCOLN

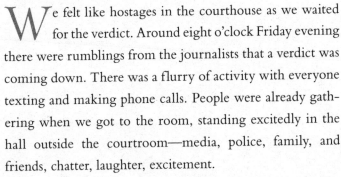

We felt like hostages in the courthouse as we waited for the verdict. Around eight o'clock Friday evening there were rumblings from the journalists that a verdict was coming down. There was a flurry of activity with everyone texting and making phone calls. People were already gathering when we got to the room, standing excitedly in the hall outside the courtroom—media, police, family, and friends, chatter, laughter, excitement.

It was odd to be gathering in Room 230 on a Friday evening. As we waited for the doors to open, the most unexpected people continued coming down the long hallway—a little disheveled, a little nervous, hushed and concerned. It was like a surprise party but without celebration—only relief and anticipation.

When the doors of the courtroom opened, we found our seats in the front row. There was a pleasant hum in the room until we heard the leg shackles rattling at 8:50 p.m. He was dressed in his suit. The reason for our gathering was not a good one. It was sobering to think what lay in the balance for the accused—a life in prison, perhaps, or freedom. The energy left the room when he took his place in the prisoner's box. I started to hear sniffles.

This was the moment we had all been waiting for.

Inevitably, when we are victimized there will also be engagement with systems designed to help. But systems don't always behave the way we want them to.

I was always worried about the criminal justice system. I had seen people come to group right after the murder of their child, and they were grieving, but they were gracious. After encountering the justice system, they turned brittle, almost unrecognizable.

I was worried when a good friend—articulate, capable, socially astute, and as strong a person as one would ever find—experienced the murder of her mother and was just entering the process of attending the preliminary hearings. I received a call from her in the late afternoon, and she was almost belligerent after spending a day in the courtroom. I was terrified of anything that could diminish her to that state.

So when our own case was before the courts I had already developed a deep-seated fear that the system could retraumatize the victims. We were caught in—and still have to deal with—the criminal justice system, and there is nothing as complex as the legal wrangling. Victims are often disappointed in the existing criminal justice system that focuses more on determining the guilt of the offender than on the victim's needs for recovery and vindication.

When this happens, when a system becomes intolerable—even abusive—do we forgive systems? Author Lewis Smedes confronts this question in his book *Forgive and Forget*. "God knows that systems can hurt people. Economic systems can lock poor people in a ghetto poverty. Political systems can turn free people into slaves. Corporate systems can push people around like puppets and toss them out like trash. But we do not forgive systems. We only forgive people."

I would maintain, however, that anything that has the capacity to treat us unjustly needs to be met with our own capacity to forgive. Most of our conflicts lie in the relationships between two people, but very quickly a conflict will find supporters, and as the conflict grows, more and more systems and people are involved. Whether they are family systems, church systems, health systems, or friendship-based systems, when a system becomes an issue in our lives or becomes dysfunctional, we need to deal with it. And when our issues poke a sleeping system and it turns on us, we can be royally victimized to the point of feeling complete powerlessness because of its immense and pervasive power. But what do we do when a system turns against us? We need patience. Systems can only work if they have our cooperation, our truth, and our goodwill.

The criminal justice system, which has been set up in

our country to protect the weak, to create justice, and to heal the victim employs some of the most skilled lawyers in our land. But when it moves against anyone, there is nothing that can stand up to the decision of the judge. It is final. Once, when I asked a judge whom he answered to, he smiled and said, "No one."

Sitting on the edge of the mount, the Nazarene sees a young lawyer in the crowd, and he raises his voice, "Blessed are the peacemakers, for they will be called children of God."

He keeps an eye on him. The lawyer stirs.

The complication of the word *peace* matches the complicated skills needed to be peacemakers and to create peace in the world around us. I think that is why this beatitude is closer to the end of the list.

What is peace? We often think that it is the absence of trouble. Instead of taking advantage of natural conflicts between people to further the dissension, we are told that it is better to intervene, to work toward peace. The culture of the day used the Hebrew word shalom, which was used sometimes to mean "quiet goodness."

According to Wil Pounds, a Baptist missionary and teacher, "Peacemakers are those disciples who strive to prevent contention and strife. However, they are not peacekeepers, but are active makers of peace. They use their influence to reconcile opposing party strife among individuals, families, churches, and the community. They change hostile attitudes to attitudes that seek the best interests of everyone."

In the victim world, misunderstandings are rampant, and the inherent contention in all of these issues gives us a unique role to either widen the gaps or narrow them. Peacemakers naturally strive for better communication and more goodwill, and they help victims procure the information they need.

Later on in the sermon, the Nazarene gives another directive to the people: "Settle matters quickly with your adversary who is taking you to court. Do it while you are still together on the way, or your adversary may hand you over to the judge, and the judge may hand you over to the officer, and you may be thrown into prison. Truly I tell you, you will not get out until you have paid the last penny."

In other words, avoid getting entangled with something too big to handle. If you are caught, at least remain disengaged emotionally. We see the Teacher doing this throughout his entire stay here on earth. He avoided the systems because our systems are imperfect and they are limited.

We need to choose when to engage. We embrace our lives and our learnings, but we need to let go of that which harms us and lures us into dysfunction. Rather than depend on systems to do justice, we need to help the justice systems by being just.

In Room 230, the defense counsel gathered around the prisoner's box. At 9:00 p.m. the judge arrived and looked over the room, a little surprised by the large number of people present. He began listing the reasons we were gathered here. He said that the jury had worked hard and had deliberated long and hard, and that we must respect their decision, whatever it was. "If anyone cannot keep their emotions in check, please leave. Please, no outburst in the court this evening."

I looked at our family; their shoes were off. I knew I didn't have to worry about them. During the months preceding the trial, our now-adult children were attending missionary training when they met a man who told them that he had received a divine message that January 17th was important. He said that they should remember that they were entering a new place. They should bring nothing into the space, nor take anything out. It was holy ground. He said it was important that they take off their shoes to help them be sensitive to everything that was happening.

He did not know that January 17 was the beginning of the trial, but we did. So we applied this message to the time in court. The message was loud and clear. We were not to see the courtroom as a place of judgment and justice, but as a sanctuary—a temple of God. It was perhaps the holy of holies. We would take off our shoes when we needed to disengage our fiery emotions and treat the courtroom as a sanctuary.

Then the jury filed in and took their places. It was different seeing them in the evening. The windows were dark. The judge looked weary. Everyone looked tired of waiting. Juror number seven stood to give the verdict. He was the tall man at the gallery end of the second row. His hands were shaking as he held the verdict.

Guilty!

That's all that mattered. Whether it was first- or second-degree murder wasn't important to me. Relief! Gratitude! It was over. I was now free of it!

Except the defense appealed the decision.

After a lengthy process, the Supreme Court of Canada overturned the provincial court's decision and ordered a retrial.

A retrial. We would have to go through it all again. I was flummoxed. I thought one trial would have been enough.

A reporter wrote, "The leave application is the first step in what could be a long legal process that may not result in Grant or the Derksen family achieving resolution for years."

The next Sunday, after hearing the appelate court's decision, I met a man who was very interested in the details of the trial, and he asked for an explanation of the appeals hearing and the court's decision. He kept asking. I kept trying to answer, but every answer just led into another question and another answer that was even less satisfactory.

Finally, he gave me an out, an acceptable pat answer: "It was a technicality."

I nodded.

He left it at that, but that didn't feel complete either. It wasn't a technicality. It was a different story that had butted up against the original story. It was a clash of stories.

This happened again and again as we met different friends. Sometimes, after settling on an easy answer, a person would pause and then, looking deeply into my eyes, would ask the question, "Did he do it?"

I would nod, "Yes." But even that would lead to the next question, and the next, and the next.

Finally we discovered that it was just too complicated to talk about. We couldn't seem to share a decent conversation with anyone about our case because it would take an insurmountable pile of words to even begin to have a conversation about it.

It was even too complicated for a book. All desire to write was gone.

I had stopped blogging.

I had stopped writing.

I had stopped.

Rather than remain stuck, I had to find another creative way to deal with this new complication. And it came. I started to paint, which launched me into a new creative venture that turned out to be a life-giving ministry for me.

I had to let go of my need for a perfect justice system and learn to reengage into an imperfect community and imperfect systems. I needed to accept brokenness.

Chapter 17

LETTING GO OF EASY RESOLUTION

One should never do wrong in return, nor mistreat any man, no matter how one has been mistreated by him.

—SOCRATES

There was a pause in the telephone conversation. Then he said, "We are delighted that you want to join us, but before you start attending, we need to ask you to do one thing."

I thought it strange that a support group for murder victims that had been phoning me for the last few months, wanting me to become part of their organization, was now backing off. I could tell this wasn't easy for him. He cleared his throat a few times, then blurted it out.

"We don't want you to talk about forgiveness," he said.

Forgiveness? They were worried about forgiveness? My forgiveness? Why were they afraid of my forgiveness? What was their concept of forgiveness?

By declaring at the press conference that we were choosing forgiveness only three days after our daughter had been found murdered, we had unexpectedly stepped into an intense universal debate. The victim community was at the center.

Recovering from an injustice is often sabotaged and infiltrated by pressures and expectations from many different sources. How do we do justice?

Victims disagree on three options for how justice should be served. The first natural response is revenge. For many, revenge might seem to be the most satisfying. It allows us a chance to see the other party suffer, and that can bring us some level of pleasure. Seeing people suffer for the wrongs they have done makes us feel that justice was dealt. Revenge doesn't always involve hurting others on a physical level. It can also lead us into actions where we want to bring harm to another's reputation, career, or family members.

Actually, the "eye for an eye" approach is becoming the dominant mood in society. We want things quickly, including our justice. We're running out of patience for just about everything. When the signal turns green, we need the person in front of us to move immediately. We need our computers to boot up faster. During rush hour, I try to be the first one out of the subway car so I don't have to wait behind all the people going up the stairs.

The second response is procedural justice, the idea of fairness in the processes that resolve disputes and allocate resources. Procedural justice concerns the fairness and the transparency of the processes by which decisions are made. This can include distributive justice (fairness in the distribution of rights or resources), retributive justice (fairness in the punishment of wrongs), and restorative justice, a more casual avenue for "making things right."

The third response is forgiveness. In this arena, forgiveness is seen as letting go of the hurt that others have caused us. Forgiveness involves compassion and means trying to adjust our vision to understand the pain and suffering of the offender that caused him or her to behave in hurtful ways. The Amish demonstrated an unforgettable act of forgiveness in October 2006 when a gunman entered one of their schools and shot ten girls, killing five. The gunman then shot himself. The community not only attended the killer's burial but also donated money to his widow and three children.

I don't want to dwell on the right and wrong of each response here, but I do want to examine the dilemma facing us when we are experiencing an injustice. Which approach should we take? The controversy, and the debate around these three, is sometimes more harmful than anything.

I have heard people referred to as good or bad victims depending on which response they choose to do justice. Whether intentionally or unintentionally, we will choose one.

At first my family and I didn't pay much attention to the debate; we were totally preoccupied with our own issues. Truthfully, it felt as if we were living on an emotional volcano that was constantly erupting inside of us; its intensity and its unexpected issues always surprised us. We were so vulnerable and so absorbed with just surviving that we didn't have much time or energy to notice the swirling forgiveness dialogue that followed us.

We felt so vulnerable and uninformed. Back then we didn't even have access to Google or any such thing. In fact, most of the literature on trauma hadn't been written yet. Besides, trauma, fear, panic, and grief don't lend themselves to quiet contemplation and learning.

Now, three years after the murder, I was very comfortable with our choice, which I thought was a personal choice, and I had no need to impose it on anyone.

So I joined the group and soon found myself in a leadership role, and I left my clichés and ghetto Christian language behind. I never doubted forgiveness as a goal and my intent; I just didn't know how to communicate it.

Glancing at the clouds, the Teacher clears his throat. "Blessed are the merciful, for they will be shown mercy."

In this setting, mercy is more than a feeling of sympathy. The Greek word for mercy is defined as a force of action; to be merciful means to be moved by compassion. If this is the case, the merciful are those who respond to human need, those who move among the suffering, those who give what they have to help those who have not.

When we are violated, the hardest thing in the world is to become merciful. We lose our empathy and generosity.

Yet we live in a world of human need. There are physical needs, emotional needs, and spiritual needs. Those who are moved by the needs of people are privileged!

In a needy world, we can easily grow calloused to people. Merciful eyes see more than surface needs. Rejection, loneliness, despair, discouragement, self-will, self-pity, fear, moral failure—these needs are not as visible, but they are real, and they are all around us. When we walk down the street, when we stroll through a mall, when we visit with neighbors, what do we see? Are our eyes open to the deeper levels of human need? Or as victims, are we too self-absorbed to see what is around us? The more mercy we give, the more we will receive.

Over the years I've become more and more convinced that we need to teach the way of forgiveness as a viable option, but the research shows that even though it is important, and people think it is important, not many know how to forgive. My search for the perfect definition of forgiveness took me right to Washington, DC.

I was invited to a prestigious roundtable discussion on forgiveness at the Hyatt Hotel. I had just begun my research in earnest and was looking for words and ideas to help crime victims heal. I thought the answer would lie in the word *forgiveness*, and that if I only found the right definition, the right sound bite, I could and would develop this wonderful program of healing and justice.

I thought I would find it at this two-day meeting of all the learned, hand-picked theologians—amazing people from across the country who were presenting papers on the topic that were later published in a book.

But as the meeting proceeded, I became quite anxious, knowing that even though the words were beautiful, nothing was in them for me personally. There was nothing for the group of crime victims at home who were awaiting my return.

Half an hour before we were to leave, someone dared to ask, "Have we defined forgiveness yet?"

The room was quiet. There were some valiant attempts to summarize the discussions, but from where I was sitting with my needs, they all fell flat and lifeless. We left unfinished.

It was still dark when I climbed into the back seat of the taxi at five o'clock the next morning, feeling miserable, dreading going home. I was slightly annoyed with myself for having booked a flight at this ridiculous hour.

"Good morning," the driver said cheerfully as I entered the back door of the cab. I settled back into the seat in a bit of a grumpy state. The driver started to chatter about all kinds of things—the hotel, the weather—but I didn't respond. I was quietly offering the occasional one-syllable answer, but nothing to encourage him. But the driver remained cheerful.

Finally he paused. "I'm sorry for talking on and on like this," he said softly, "but you are the first sober fare I've had all night."

I apologized. I told him I hadn't had my coffee. I told

him that I had been disappointed in the conference. I just wanted to go home and be with my family.

He nodded. He said he understood. Apparently my accent gave me away, so he asked me a little bit about Canada.

When he found out I worked with homicide issues, he seemed pleasantly interested. So I asked him why Washington, DC, where he lived, had the highest rate of murder in all of North America.

He fell silent for a long moment. Then he said, "My brothers are still angry because of the years of slavery, the racism in this country, and the poverty. This anger shows itself in violence."

Even though he was identifying with his people, describing great sorrow and pain, I couldn't help but notice that he spoke with no anger and absolutely no bitterness. He wasn't edgy. In the dark, he seemed to glow with some inner joy and sunshine.

I couldn't resist. I asked him the burning question. "I can tell that you aren't angry. Why not?"

Without missing a beat, he said. "I believe in forgiveness."

My heart stopped.

"What of forgiveness?" I asked.

Without any further prompting, he talked about forgiveness with an eloquence I hadn't ever heard before or since. He talked about the beauty of being set free, of letting go of the past, embracing the moment, and anticipating the future.

By this time, the sun was beginning to rise. The sunrise seemed so symbolic of what was happening in the car. The light was flooding in.

In his simple terms, he was able to describe what we had failed to do in the previous two days. He not only described forgiveness, but he also radiated the word.

By the time I reached the airport, I felt like a new person.

I knew then that forgiveness doesn't need to be defined to be lived and felt.

———————

I had to let go of my hope of easy answers.
I had to accept the difficulty of choosing
a way that would not make sense.

———————

Chapter 18

Letting Go of My Self-Pity

There is a hard law. When an injury is done to us, we never recover until we forgive.

—Alan Paton

Self-pity becomes your oxygen. But you learned to breathe it without a gasp. So, nobody even notices you're hurting.

—Paul Monette

Self-pity is easily the most destructive of the non-pharmaceutical narcotics; it is addictive, gives momentary pleasure and separates the victim from reality.

—John Gardner

The first summer after the murder, I took videos for Camp Arnes, the camp where my husband worked as program director. It was a good job; it took me outdoors, challenged my skill, and let me see the whole camp. One of my assignments was to videotape Camp Seton, their rugged ranch camp in the Carberry Hills, two hours west of Winnipeg.

I'm afraid of horses, so I managed to get Cliff to come with me for two days. I would videotape, and he would take photos with our 35mm camera. He should have been the one shooting the video; he was a much better, more experienced photographer than I was. But it was my summer assignment, and he didn't want to interfere other than to remind me to check my settings, suggest new camera angles, and help me carry the heavy equipment.

Camp Seton, exceptionally beautiful and situated along a river, was even more beautiful through a lens. We had a lot of fun experimenting and taking sunset shots on a cliff that was appropriately called Inspiration Point, overlooking the river. We tried some tricky photography in one spot where the campers looked as if they were jumping dangerously off a cliff into thin air, but they landed safely on a pile of soft sand right below.

I especially liked the way the camp was laid out. The horses were fenced down in a valley, surrounded by the tents. No matter what we did, we could always see those gorgeous animals moving gracefully in their corral.

The camp director had planned a chuck wagon ride for us to photograph at the end of our second day. The lighting was perfect, and it promised to be even better with a full moon rising.

The director started harnessing the horses, but I didn't like the feel of it. The kids were hyper, and the huge Clydesdale horses were fidgety. I was fidgety.

It was taking them awhile to get set up, so Cliff and I went on ahead. The plan was that we would open the barbed wire gate for them, videotape them as they came down the dusty trail, and then once they were through the gate, we would get on and videotape from the wagon.

We went down the hill and wandered around, looking for the perfect angle. The winding trail lent itself to the classic S-curve picture. Cliff wanted to stand right in the open and take a shot straight on; I wanted to find bushes to hide behind. I said it was because I wanted to frame the picture with some leaves, but in actuality, it was a precaution. I had stood in the open with the trail horses, and every time they had seen me and heard my video camera humming, they had shied away from me. I had a lot of video footage of horses shying away from the camera. But those were small horses compared to those pulling the wagon. I didn't want to spook them, and I wasn't about to put a whole wagon full of kids in jeopardy.

The bushes I found didn't lend themselves to what I wanted. I was just about to look for some others when I heard a strange sound.

Cliff called to me, "I think they're coming … and they're out of control!"

He was right. I glanced up just in time to see them come streaking over the hill. I ducked. I thought I was probably safe right where I was, hidden behind some bushes behind the fence. Surely they'd stay on the trail. They wouldn't run through the fence!

That was naive. They could run through a fence. I had heard stories. So just in case, I stood up slowly.

The team was veering off the road and heading right for me! I was in a small ditch, and I could see those huge hooves pounding up the dust at eye level and the camp director desperately pulling at the reins. I had seconds, but seconds can feel like a long time.

My past didn't cross my mind. Instead, I saw a bit of my present and mostly the future. If I stayed where I was, I could go to be with Candace.

The hooves were thundering towards me. I kept thinking, *This can't be happening. This only happens in the movies.* It would be over in a moment. If I just stayed in that spot, it would all be over. Oh, how I yearned for the promise of those words.

But I jumped—just in time. I felt the horses rush past me. Then I remembered the barbed wire fence and raised my arms to protect my neck and face. I could feel the wire slash across my arms as I was hurled to the ground.

I lay twisted on the ground; I couldn't move because I was tangled up in a mess of video cords and barbed wire. I heard Cliff yelling, and I wondered vaguely if he was angry because I hadn't taken pictures or hadn't stopped the horses. Then I saw Cliff's face, his relief, and I knew that he hadn't been yelling out of anger. "Oh, thank God," he kept saying as he gently untangled me.

The video camera was fine except for one distinct souvenir scratch on the camera case. The director and the one camper left in the wagon weren't hurt. The wagon had lodged behind two trees, and once the horses had shaken off their harnesses, they had begun to graze.

I was bruised and scratched, but the only casualty was my cheap watch, which had been smashed by the barbed wire slashing at my wrists.

I knew that I couldn't fool myself anymore. I didn't want to die. I had just proven to myself and everyone else that I wanted to live very much. I had chosen to be with my family and not with Candace, and I felt guilty. Candace needed me, yet I had chosen life.

No, I knew I was wrong. Candace had needed me that winter night. She didn't need me anymore. My family needed me more. Whether I wanted it to or not, life would go on. I needed to adjust. I needed to learn how to live again.

After the terrorist attack on the World Trade Center on September 11, 2001, it was reported in the newspaper that the general public came to Ground Zero just to look. They would stand for long periods of time, staring at the grotesquely twisted iron and rubble. This trance-like stare has been well documented.

The cumulative effects of fragmentation, traumatization, disorientation, disempowerment, and unsatisfactory closure can cause a paralysis of self-pity. Self-pity can be remarkably self-sustaining, particularly in conjunction with depression or other conditions. However, self-pity is a way of paying attention to oneself, albeit negatively; it is a means of self-soothing or self-nurturing ("I hurt so much").

How do we get unstuck?

Just prior to Candace's disappearance, I had read a book that had an enormous influence on me and seemed to prepare me for what was about to happen. It was Viktor Frankl's book, *Man's Search for Meaning.* I always keep it close.

Frankl was an Austrian neurologist and psychiatrist, as well as a Holocaust survivor, who emphasized again and again that we might not have a choice over a lot of things, and he was speaking from some dire situations. From this very place, he wrote, "Everything can be taken from a man but one thing: the last of the human freedoms—to choose one's attitude in any given set of circumstances, to choose one's own way."

After a busy day, Cliff and I met at a central location in the city for a quick supper before going to the theatre. It was very cold. Even the restaurant felt cold and not as welcoming as usual.

It was also a slow night in the restaurant, only two other couples that I could see. One couple, sitting almost directly across from us, ate rather quickly and left. I noticed them particularly because of the woman's stylish hair color and unusual cut. What could have been a disaster on almost anyone else gave her an air of artistic sophistication that I couldn't help but admire.

The other couple was sitting farther back. She had lovely gray hair, and she smiled as we passed them. I wondered vaguely if they recognized us from the news.

Getting ready to leave, I went to the washroom. As I was washing my hands, the woman with the lovely gray hair entered and immediately approached me. "Are you Wilma Derksen?" she whispered tentatively, politely.

I nodded.

"I'm going to cry …" she said, as her eyes welled up with tears.

We just hugged—two strangers in the washroom. Two mothers knowing what it meant. She had lost a son to suicide.

"But I can't believe you are smiling," she said. "I can't believe you can still laugh."

It was what I needed—affirmation that we were heading in the right direction.

I'm not sure what I said. I think I might have just shrugged my shoulders. "Life is bizarre. What can we do?" And I smiled some more. I remember she was smiling as I left.

I found my husband standing off to the side by the wall, looking a little confused.

He beckoned to me. "I have to tell you something. That couple across from us …"

I nodded. "The stylish couple, unique hairdo?" I thought that they had left much earlier, but apparently they hadn't.

"They paid for us. When the man offered, I told him that it was for two of us, and it might be more than he expected. But he insisted anyway. I didn't know what to do—just thanked him—still kind of protesting. Then his wife joined him, and she said, 'We are praying for you.' Imagine that … they are praying for us."

We both stood there trying to take it all in—aghast, shaken, feeling guilty, happy, bewildered, and cherished. Then gratitude. Gratitude is the last powerful light that drives away the darkness.

Two couples—four strangers—had just stepped into our life and made it better for us, and then disappeared without waiting to be thanked.

We walked out into the night to find our car—a frozen block of steel and glass. Yet Winnipeg felt warm.

Pure, beautiful gratitude!

I had to let go of my self-pity and
my right to feel sorry for myself.

Chapter 19

LETTING GO OF CLOSURE

There is hope in forgiveness.

—JOHN PIPER

" For this I think I might need a special bouquet of flowers when the jury returns with their verdict," I wrote in my blog the morning of the last day of the trial. I continued:

> There is nothing like the gift of a wildflower bouquet that openly expresses freedom and abandonment. There is nothing like a bouquet of spring flowers—yellow daffodils, crocuses, or elegant tulips. I love the simplicity of the daisy, the drama of the Gerbera flower, the frilliness of carnations.
>
> But there is one flower that stands alone—the rose. The soft, silky feel of a fresh rose petal evokes tenderness; the fragrant scent of a spring rose brings refreshment; the vibrant colors of red, pink, peach, purple, orange, yellow, and white roses remind us of the dazzling beauty of creation; and getting pricked by a thorn causes pain. Roses are a reflection of life.
>
> I think my personal love of roses started with

watching my grandfather care for his rose garden. I watched how he would admire and caress them daily. They grew for him. The colors convey different messages; all of the messages are timely. Every color encourages us to live more fully.

But for this occasion I think I will choose the white rose. The pure white rose symbolizes truth and innocence. It also says, "I miss you" and "You are heavenly." White speaks to me of the grief of her passing, her purity—our purity before God. White roses fill me with the serenity of holiness.

Regardless of the verdict, I am going to lay down twenty-six white roses on Candace's grave in the cemetery—and cry. There will be a rose for every year that she has been gone. The white rose will be like putting a fresh white piece of paper into the typewriter, like stepping onto a white field of snow, or like spreading a white tablecloth on the dining room table.

What we call the beginning is often the end. And to make an end is to make a beginning. The end is where we start from.

I wrote this terrified of the ending—or would it be a non-ending?

Someone had told me that the day after the murder trial for her sister, her world had crumbled. She hadn't been prepared for the stillness of the ending of a process that had really not brought the closure everyone anticipated.

I had felt some of that already after the preliminary

hearing when, the day after, I had sat and stared at the wall, too tired to call a friend, too lonely to stay with myself, too disappointed to feel any hope, and too weary to get on with life.

I was going to fill this ending with roses.

A friend entered the courtroom with a rose. "I want this to be the first," she said.

"Did you read my blog?"

"Yes. I read it," she confessed.

I hugged her.

Not wanting the rose to be seen by the jury as some kind of message, I simply stuck it into my daughter's crocheting bag behind my chair—out of sight but not out of mind.

As we were going for lunch, my daughter noticed the rose in her bag. "Should I take it with me to the room?" she asked.

"Not yet." For some reason, I wanted the rose to stay with me in the courtroom for the entire time we were listening to the summations and judge's charge. I wanted its short life to mean something.

For the rest of the day, I left it on an unused chair to the side. At the end of the long day, I noticed the rose still on the chair, looking completely wilted. It had spent its life to comfort me. It was done.

I regretted not finding water for it. Not willing to part with it, I took it to the family room with me, poured water into a tiny coffee cup, and propped it up against a cup dispenser at the back of the kitchenette counter.

Three days later—after waiting patiently for the jury to

arrive at a verdict—when we returned to our tiny room, I noticed that the white rose had fully revived. I touched a petal to express my gratitude, to love it. Not only had it survived, it seemed to have grown in its beauty, opening slowly in radiant splendor. It gave me such comfort. It was a piece of serenity. I stared at it for quite a while.

Why was it so alive?

Outside that courthouse there was a fierce storm. I went to watch it at the window, the tumultuous wind whipping up the snow into a frenzy.

There was also a fierce debate going on at the far end of the building where a jury of twelve was cloistered away, discussing in detail all the evidence that they had heard during the last five weeks.

The questions in my mind seemed almost interchangeable with the ones I was faced with twenty-six years ago when it all started, on a stormy winter night.

There was a fierce battle raging inside me. It also was raging in the hearts of my friends and family who had joined us.

It seems there are situations in life when the only satisfactory response is a violent storm. Yet all I wanted was for it all to end so we could have peace.

Ambiguity causes confusion, sucks up time, keeps us from taking action, and leaves us with an unpleasant taste in our mouths. It is a nagging item on our "to do" list that we just can't ever seem to cross off.

Victims yearn to find closure and a way of moving on, but the aftermath of violence won't let us. For us, closure describes a time when all the ends are tied, when all the issues are resolved, the truth fully disclosed, and the person murdered restored to us. That would be closure.

Each of the issues that I have described in the previous chapters are in and of themselves a good reason for this lack of closure. Our story is fragmented, our minds can't forget, uncontrolled emotion can be triggered at any moment, and there's an ongoing relationship with the perpetrator. In our case, it has been an off-and-on relationship for thirty-one years, all connected to the justice systems in one form or another.

We live in a constant state of waiting. Closure remains elusive, and so does the permission to get on with life.

As the sun climbs, the mountainside becomes warmer. The Nazarene's voice starts to sound dry. Someone hands him a flask of water. After taking a drink, he continues, "Blessed are those who hunger and thirst for righteousness, for they will be filled."

He has the crowd's attention. They have been fighting their unfulfilled desires, and now the Master is saying that they are privileged to have strong, persistent yearnings. It is a good thing to want something. There is nothing as compelling as hunger and thirst.

The desire for closure can also be extremely strong. We want the stress to stop. We want it to end.

The Nazarene gives permission to be desirous. It isn't

the desire that is wrong most often, it is the things that we want that are bad for us. To want justice as a victim of violence is not wrong. To have things set right and for goodness to win is not wrong. It is what the entire universe wants and aches to achieve.

But he is talking about a different kind of desire, a holy one. The desire for righteousness. What is righteousness? It is a moral state of perfection. But righteousness takes time to achieve, a lifetime to achieve, so to become obsessed with closure is counterproductive. Life isn't about closures; it is about chapter endings and new beginnings, challenging beginnings that give us one more time to get it right.

While everyone was waiting at the elevator, I did what I always do when I leave a motel room. I do a final sweep of the room to see what my children have left behind. Even though they are adults now, it is a hard habit to break. It's interesting how many personal belongings we had brought into the Law Courts Building. The room was empty except for two garbage bins filled to the brim with all kinds of cartons of take-out food. The chairs were a little askew, so I straightened them.

Then I noticed the single rose standing on the window sill. It had been moved from behind the cup dispenser to the window that faced the Remand Center, still in the tiny cup of water. It stood tall, regal, as only a long-stemmed white rose can do—a lonely gesture of love against the dark night.

For one moment I wondered about taking it with me. The duffel bags were already packed and gone. I had nothing to wrap the rose in. Without protection, it would never survive the freezing temperatures of the night. But I still couldn't throw it away. More than ever, I now needed it close to me for comfort. I grabbed it and headed for the doors.

The journalists were waiting for us. It seemed a million lights started flashing as we opened the front doors of the Law Courts Building. I know I should have expected it, but there is really no way to prepare oneself for a moment like that.

They asked us questions and, as usual, I fumbled for the right words. Then one of the reporters asked me, "Why are you holding a white rose?"

I looked down. Yes, I was holding the rose.

Should I tell them? Should I tell them that I was cleaning up the room, grabbing what was left behind, and then simply forgot to pack it. I was holding a rose, but it could have been anything that had been left behind. Yet now, holding the white rose, it seemed so appropriate for the moment. I had been so worried about finding the right words—the right sound bite for that impossible moment—and there it was in my hand.

A white rose is worth a thousand words.

The news report stated:

Outside court, an emotional Cliff and Wilma Derksen said they often wondered whether their journey for

justice would ever end. "I think the jury was tremen-
dously courageous," said Wilma, wiping her eyes while
clutching a fresh white rose in her hands. She plans to
lay the flower at Candace's headstone in a private family
service Saturday morning. "It's a symbol of innocence,
purity, love and fresh beginnings," she said. "The way
this story has come together has completed us."

It wasn't the end—only a chapter break, and we had to
be satisfied with that. This rose followed us to Ottawa. The
story didn't end here, nor has it ended even as I write. We
are facing a retrial. It's now thirty-two years since Candace
disappeared, and in a way it is starting all over.

Rather than fussing over this new development, I see
another opportunity to learn. Obviously, I haven't learned
it all yet.

*I had to let go of my dream of closure and
live in a process. I had to live in the now.*

Chapter 20

THE NEVER-ENDING PROCESS, STAGE ONE

> *True forgiveness is when you can say, "Thank*
> *you for that experience."*
>
> —OPRAH WINFREY

She came into my office, a beautiful woman vibrating with energy.

"I want to forgive," she said vehemently. "I hate having these feelings, so I want to get rid of them. And I want to do it quickly."

At a recent house party, she had found her husband sitting on the bottom step with his iPhone. From her position she could read the text on his phone and knew immediately that her husband was having an affair.

Even though she was completely devastated, she never let on to her husband or anyone else at the party. She just carried on as if nothing had happened. She carried on this act for at least a week before she was able to find the space to confront her husband.

Even now, though she was shaking like a leaf, she was direct, efficient, and brave, her intentions clear. "What is the process? And how do I do it quickly?"

She wanted to get over it quickly before anyone else found out about it. She didn't want her children or her extended family to know.

She looked so desperate, so very unhappy.

I've been asked this question a lot over the years. Some come to me wanting the formula for someone else. Frantic people want to move through the pain quickly. They see forgiveness as the answer but think it is a single action. When it doesn't seem to work, they become desperate.

It's always the same. Give me a quick fix!

Letting go isn't easy. It isn't a one-time decision. It is a long process, and even though it is integral to forgiveness, it doesn't end there. The process itself is the most important part of the pain of being wounded in the first place. It is the learning, growing, accepting of reality, of loss, of pain.

But now I would like to place it in a larger context of forgiveness that I have followed and refined for myself over the years.

Our experience forced us to approach forgiveness in two stages. The first stage was informed by not knowing who the offender was. For twenty-three years, we were faced with forgiving a catastrophic event with no known perpetrator.

Some wondered out loud in my presence whether forgiveness was an accurate response in our case, since it wasn't interpersonal. According to them, forgiveness was personal, a way of dealing with a person with whom you had a conflict. I wondered with them.

As I read books about forgiveness, I was often frustrated because none of them seemed to come close to dealing with the issue I was facing: forgiving an offender who was unknown to me.

Yet since forgiveness was synonymous with freedom for me, I wasn't about to allow anyone to take it away from me.

I kept working at it, forming it as I went. I would describe the process as an overarching mindset of surrender. And it doesn't need to involve anyone else. It is basically an autonomous forgiveness, a method of forgiveness that we can do alone, without any thought of mending or fixing a relationship.

It is a way of dealing with a conflict without a known perpetrator, offender, or injurer. It is a process to avoid getting caught in the pitfalls of trauma and to tap into the transformational forgiveness process in its purest form.

Notice my emphasis on process.

Surrendipity Forgiveness is a phrase I've coined for that overarching mindset that we adopted after our daughter was murdered. It combines the word *surrender*, which means to stop resisting and submit to the reality of a situation, and the word *serendipity*, which is the ability to find something valuable or agreeable in everything.

It was probably too soon to go back to work, but we needed the money. Within half a year after Candace disappeared, I was hired as western regional editor for a national church paper. I was so relieved and excited to finally be writing full time. My first assignment was to attend a national conference in Saskatchewan with a colleague and report on it—nothing too demanding.

But when I was introduced to one of the conference leaders as the journalist for the event, he quickly recognized my name. "I would love it if you said a few words to the delegates," he said, "and tell your story tomorrow at the opening."

When I hesitated, he quickly added. "They have been praying for your family. They would love to hear how you are doing."

What he didn't know was that I wasn't doing that well. The next day was Candace's birthday, the first anniversary of her birth since her murder. I was terrified of the day. I didn't know how I was going to survive it because every time I thought about it, I would burst into tears and feel as if my heart was literally breaking.

How could I get up in front of a church full of people and say anything? I couldn't even say no to the man at that moment, because to decline meant I would have to give a reason, and if I even mentioned Candace's name, I was sure I would dissolve into a really messy crying bout that I wasn't sure I would be able to control. Besides, my colleague was standing right there, and I needed to be professional.

I couldn't do it. I just couldn't! It was too much to ask of a mother!

I somehow got out of making a final commitment.

In my room, processing it, I knew that I wanted to say no—and would have said no—but the feelings of anger and frustration signalled to me that something bigger was afoot, and I had promised myself that I would forgive. I wouldn't make decisions out of anger, frustration, and self-protection.

What did forgiveness look like in this situation? I needed to unpack all of it. I needed to address my resistance and my frustration.

Besides, it was a chance to tell my story, and telling the story was important.

I mentioned in the beginning that letting go means we close the door, even nail it shut, and deliberately turn around. Once we truly find acceptance, we can move forward toward forgiveness. We then must embrace our story the way it is now. I even suggest dramatizing the injustice. I use the word *dramatize* because it allows for us to play with the story, to look at it in many different ways.

There are so many ways to tell our story, and the more ways we do it, the more we learn. We can tell just the facts: who, what, where, when, how, like a journalist. We can tell it as a grievance story, where we as central players are the innocent victims. We can tell it as a story of the struggle between good and evil, blowing it up into epic proportions. We can tell it in fictional form or as a documentary. There are a million ways to tell our story, and all of them are valid.

Leo Widrich confirms this. "Our brains become more active when we tell stories," he writes. "When we are being told a story, things change dramatically. Not only are the language processing parts in our brain activated, but any other area in our brain that we would use when experiencing the events of the story are too." He continues, "We are wired that way. A story, if broken down into the simplest form, is a connection of cause and effect. And that is exactly how we think. We think in narratives all day long, no matter if it is about buying groceries, whether we think about work or our spouse at home. We make up (short) stories in our heads for every action and conversation."

In the middle of the night as I tossed and turned, I gave myself grace. It is natural for a mother to want to grieve the death of her first child privately on the anniversary of her birth.

There were also professional reasons why I didn't want to go onstage. I was to cover the conference from an objective journalist's point of view. To take the platform meant I was inserting myself into the story. This was unprofessional—except that my colleague had seen no harm in it. In fact, he had seemed somewhat amused and pleased with it all.

"Let it go—just do it."

Besides, I would learn something. Edward Hall, an anthropologist, says, "Humans are the learning organism par excellence. The drive to learn is as strong as the sexual drive—and it begins earlier and lasts longer." Peter Senge writes, "Real learning gets to the heart of what it means to be human. Through learning we re-create ourselves. Through learning we become able to do something we never were able to do. Through learning we reperceive the world and our relationship to it. Through learning we extend our capacity to create, to be part of the generative process of life."

Each situation that we encounter is a huge opportunity to learn. We spend a great deal of money and time learning many things to give us more equity in life. Yet we often avoid the greatest teacher of all: life's challenges that are uniquely ours.

Our trauma can become our teacher.

Perhaps by appearing onstage, I might even be helping someone else to face their ordeals. I had promised that I would use the experience I was going through for good.

At Candace's funeral—funerals are a great place to learn as we face our mortality—we were reminded that the next challenge in dealing with a negative experience, especially something like murder, was to overcome it with good.

What is goodness? It is a euphemism for God, actually. It is commonly used to describe something desirable, reliable, welcome; the inner quality of moral excellence, virtue, kindness, generosity, and the best part, strength.

There is nothing that takes the wind out of an evil act like an equivalent act of goodness. The tension is neutralized; the aggression has been met with the perfect defense. In the face of an assault of accusations and negativity, it is so easy to succumb to the negativity and meet it with negativity in kind. But an invasion of kindness and loving words filled with understanding and beauty will cut the power of the negativity.

In the face of something that is life-taking, the challenge is to live even more fiercely. There is nothing more life-giving than a spirit of joy and peace and wonderful good works and good words.

The next morning I said yes.

I got up in front of all those people, and I told them my story briefly. I told them how much we appreciated their prayers in the past and would relish them in the future.

I could feel the tears. I could feel Candace—very close, dangerously close. The entire time, I felt I was on the precipice of an emotional volcano, but I managed to get through it.

When I stepped off the stage I was greeted with hugs and prayers.

At the end of the day, I had been so showered with lovely words and blessings that I went to my room that night and, instead of facing the demons of grief, I was filled with love and support.

What I had thought was going to be a huge sacrifice on my part turned out to be my healing.

I was thankful I had taken the plunge.

Speaking in public after that became easier and easier. In fact, in hindsight, I think it became my way of doing therapy.

This incident was only one of the more minor challenges that I continued to face for the next twenty-three years before we knew the offender.

The issues we faced weren't about the offender; they were more about the hurt and pain of the aftermath of murder.

Every time I felt the flash of anger, I knew there was some hurt that I needed to uncover, examine, and transform into something good so I would be filled with, rather than depleted of, all joy.

It seemed like a constant struggle.

The Nazarene continues to unpack the principle of for-giveness as he travels with his companions around the countryside. When one of his students asks him, "Lord how many times shall I forgive my brother or sister who sins against me? Up to seven times?" Jesus answered, "I tell you, not just seven times, but seventy-seven times."

That's *surrendipity*. That's forgiveness: when our hearts are more full than they are empty.

Chapter 21

THE NEVER-ENDING PROCESS, STAGE TWO

The telephone rang. It was a distant voice from the past—a Catholic priest who had become important to our group of parents of murdered children.

We chatted a bit, catching up.

Then he said he had something to ask me.

Without his saying another word, I knew what it would be about.

I was remembering the first time I heard about this man—sometime in 1989—four years after Candace's murder, and about the time I was beginning to face my new identity as the parent of a murdered child.

As a member of the organizing board of Family Survivors of Homicide, one of my first assignments was to visit a woman who had indicated she wanted to join our support group. According to the president, she had sounded a little desperate to meet with other parents of murdered children and was extremely disappointed that the meeting had been cancelled due to a snowstorm.

However, when I heard about her loneliness, I decided

that I would battle my way through the blizzard to the south end of the city to meet her in a coffee shop not far from her place. She seemed so relieved to see me.

It was at this meeting that I heard her story for the first time. It became an important story for me. She had immigrated from war-torn Ireland in the late 1960s to work as a lay missionary, met her future husband here in Winnipeg, married him, and had two wonderful sons. On a chilly Sunday afternoon on her way home from church, she decided to pick up two items from the store for Sunday dinner. Her sons remained in the car. They were playing the Beatles on the tape deck. According to a witness, a young teenager appeared out of nowhere, hopped into the running car, and started to drive. When the two boys fought with him, the teen fought them off. In desperation, one son jumped out, but the car was already moving. He was caught under the wheels and was killed.

The teenager continued, driving wildly through town, causing about seven accidents in his attempt to elude the police. The teen was caught and tried in court a year later. He was charged with second-degree murder, but a plea bargain brought the charges down to manslaughter. He was given three years.

Later, as part of our group, this mother continued to unpack her story for us. With the aid of her parish priest, she was given the opportunity to meet the young offender.

I remember her describing the meeting with him. They talked for two hours. At the end, she told the young offender that she did not wish him ill. All she wanted was for him never to cause anybody else any trauma and for him to try to do something positive with his life.

Later, when I finally met with the priest, he told me that the young offender had changed, and that the mother's visit had done a world of good.

I also knew from her that the visit had given her something important. She found it hard to describe the impact, but I could tell that it had given her some answers, given her a role, and released her from the ongoing trauma of murder. For this, she continued to be grateful to this wonderful priest.

Back then, it was this story that motivated me to explore other programs that brought offenders and victims together. Our public decision to forgive also opened up doors for me in the growing restorative justice movement.

Now the priest was calling me. He had received a call from someone in Corrections wondering whether he would be open to giving Grant a bed.

A bed?

I asked him quickly whether he was now a director of a halfway house. He said no, he was retired but living in a residence that did have beds that could be used to give someone a second chance. He was in charge of a house largely used for retired priests. I paused.

He wondered what I would advise him to do.

I wanted to know: Did he believe Grant guilty of killing Candace? As someone who had been approached to be a supervisor of a dangerous offender, if he thought the offender innocent then I knew that he would be ill equipped to manage a sexual offender of this caliber.

He hesitated, then confessed that he couldn't even remember the offender's name. So I told him—Mark Edward Grant. He then also expressed doubts about his ability to take on something like this, given his age.

There was one more thing the priest had told me during our telephone conversation. He told me that Grant had converted.

Mark Edward Grant was now a born-again believer.

I had heard about another time when Grant had become a believer—and that was before the trial, where I had seen no evidence of a spiritual man. I suggested that I would believe that Grant was sincere only if he confessed to the murder.

After I hung up the telephone, the thought of Grant's conversion stuck with me, niggling at me.

I didn't tell Cliff immediately. I kept the conversation on hold until the right time.

Stella's has great food, a homey ambiance, and is perfect for casual dining. We chose a table in the middle of the patio. The evening was warm—not too hot, not too cold. No mosquitoes. Beside us, a lush brown-eyed Susan was climbing up a wooden obelisk. All around us the patio fence was thickly covered with vines. There were some potted plants. Light jazz was playing in the background.

We ordered wine—red for me, white for Cliff.

Cliff leaned forward. "Now tell me all about the priest."

After relaying the entire story, Cliff leaned back. "I

would like to meet with him," he said. "Especially if now he claims to be a believer."

I was stunned. I told Cliff that the priest had been realistic about the conversion and expressed doubt about such claims. Cliff nodded but was unshaken. "I would like to meet with him."

There it was again—that thought! The thought that pursued us for thirty years: Would you meet with him?

It was a question that had emerged in conversation with others shortly after Cliff and I had declared that we would forgive. Even when we didn't know who the person was, it had always emerged in my question-and-answer times after a presentation.

Actually, there were three questions that seemed to follow me. The first one was about Cliff. It would start with, "How is he doing?" But if I pursued it, they were really wondering if we were still together. The second question was about my children, "How are they doing?" I think that they were really asking how the murder affected our parenting. It had a huge effect on us but, miraculously, our two children turned out to be wonderful, contributing people, admired by many. The third question was regarding the murderer and our public statement that we wanted to forgive. Had we really forgiven? When I said that I would forgive him, they would ask, "Would you meet with him?" It seemed to be the test of our forgiveness.

I offered Cliff a reality check. I carefully outlined all the apparent problems of such a meeting. The case is before the courts—there would be legal considerations. There would be publicity. People would want to record it, etc.

"But what if we could?" Cliff insisted. "What if we could do it safely, confidentially, with someone we trust?" With the priest in the picture, it felt safer somehow.

It was a new thought for me as well. What if we could have a confidential meeting with Grant—no one knowing, no possibility of interfering with justice, just us and him—to ask him questions?

"Would you?" Cliff asked.

The world stopped. The question was real to us— imagined, but real.

I knew that for the years following the murder, I had wanted desperately to meet the abductor to find out what he had done and why. After Grant's arrest, I wanted a confession. Now, it was different. What did I want? I would want to hear his story. I am always interested in the story, and I knew I would be particularly interested in his.

I remembered the three questions people were constantly asking—especially the third one. Did our meeting have anything to do with forgiveness? Not much. Contrary to what others thought, I had never equated meeting him with forgiveness. Forgiveness was something we did in the privacy of our hearts—letting go and choosing love. Forgiveness doesn't mean condoning murder. It doesn't mean ignoring the wrong.

Would I like to meet with him? The question was there waiting. "Yes." I answered slowly. I would like a face-to-face conversation. Even if Grant would never admit to killing Candace, I would still like to hear him explain his life to me.

Cliff ordered a lovely cheesecake topped with strawberries for dessert, and we sipped our coffee as we lingered over this imaginary visit—talking about it, continuing to imagine it, even relishing it as a possibility for the moment, living it, and wondering what we would discover.

As I continued to think about my answer, I was acutely aware of Candace. I was aware of my own feelings. I sank deep into my heart, my mother's heart.

Both of us knew that the real question wasn't whether we had forgiven. I knew we had. The underlying question for us was this: How do you know if someone has truly changed?

Would meeting him give us that answer?

Forgiveness is love. Love is responsible, patient, and wise. I know that I cannot love only the people in prison; I also need to love the vulnerable children on the street. To open the prison gates and let someone like Grant out when I am so convinced of his guilt makes me culpable. Love is careful and prevents further harm.

And then I knew my ultimate question of him, the man who took our daughter's life. I would simply ask, "After spending so much time in the institution, do you still have the ability to love?"

◀

The Nazarene, betrayed by his best friend, had to know how important the answer to this one question was.

"Do you love me?" he asks Peter three times—the exact number of times Peter had betrayed him.

Underlying the obvious question are the hidden questions. "Can you take responsibility for what you did? Can you turn your fear into love? Are we going to be safe with you? Will you love us?"

Peter is unsure at first—probably surprised that his motivation rather than his actions were under the microscope. He also knew that this wasn't a shallow question; it was a question about a love that endures, that sacrifices, and that looks deep to find and touch the very core of one's being.

"Do you love me?"

It is ultimately the only question.

It is the ultimate test. It is directed at us as well. Can we love?

As we left the restaurant, we walked out together touching hands. I noticed the waiter smiling. Love is the only way I know to deal with this mortal coil, this endless story that continues to wind itself around us, that doesn't seem to have an end.

The second part of forgiveness is interpersonal: forgiving the offender. This is the common understanding of forgiveness. We were introduced to this forgiveness in a new way when a stranger to us was charged with the first-degree murder of our daughter. After twenty-three years, we had already worked at forgiveness in a *surrendipity* way. I actually think this was helpful in many ways. But another question came to us: How does forgiveness apply to a murderer? Is murder too big to forgive? Is it even forgivable?

It all took time to process. Forgiveness takes time.

Research shows that this inclination to choose quickly, and sometimes harshly, has its roots in our belief in scarcity. Either/or thinking maintains the myth that resources are finite and that our very survival depends on getting our piece of the pie.

It is a place of survival—a place of negativity.

So rather than go to this negative place, when I forgive I am challenging myself and everyone who supports us to find another way of looking at it, another place to sit and be.

Compassion is taken from the Latin word meaning "co-suffering." Compassion is a positive, life-giving place, a virtue.

Compassion is the essence of community. Without it, we cannot heal ourselves or our relationships.

Thomas Merton writes, "The whole idea of compassion is based on a keen awareness of the interdependence of all these living beings, which are all part of one another, and all involved in one another."

Even the word feels warm, comfortable, and safe.

Compassion is the only word that has sustained me over the last twenty-six years. I hope it will continue to sustain.

The very first step in forgiving anyone is to make sure that the person you are forgiving is actually the offender, the person who committed the injury. It isn't always easy to name your enemy. It had taken me thirty years to find out who had killed our daughter—and to be convinced.

I remember talking to a couple who had lost their child

in a criminally negligent accident. You would think it would be quite obvious who the person was who had victimized their family. Even the courts were clear about this. But the woman blamed her husband for it all.

Many victims blame the police or the system for the injustice, rather than the actual offender. In couples' disputes, it is important to remember that the person who is acting out a dysfunction might not be the one who is actually instigating it. We need to sort out whom we blame and for what.

So often we think that forgiveness needs to be worked out immediately with the person who has offended us. We need to make friends.

Actually, our amazing teacher on forgiveness, the Nazarene, didn't do it this way. When his best friend became a force against him, he simply said, "Get behind me, Satan." The words "behind me" means that he's moving forward. He was saying, "My dear friend, you are working against me at this moment. You need to be behind me or beside me, but not in front of me right now." After their disagreement, the Nazarene went back to Peter and made things right. Similarly, when someone moves against us, we need to first disengage emotionally, physically, mentally, and verbally.

The Nazarene reacted to his opposition like this many times. He did it physically. Often we read about how he went up into the mountains at the end of the day. He left all the stressors behind. Eventually he disconnected from his opposition intellectually by talking in parables. He started to use language that they couldn't attack. He disengaged.

When we disengage, we have the opportunity to resist acting out of revenge. We can be objective about the conflict and begin to think strategically about how to solve the problem.

Remembering the conversation we had with a parent of a murdered child that first night, I remembered that our true enemy wasn't Grant—he had never posed any physical threat to the rest of us then or now. Our true enemy was the aftermath of murder.

We could disengage from him.

Once we have disengaged, then and only then can we assess how much control we have in a situation, because that is all that we can change or address in a relationship.

I remember the first time we were reminded exactly how much influence we had in the trial process. We had planned out our lives to make space to attend the trial, which took some doing. Then we received a call from a lawyer for the Crown telling us that the trial was being postponed for possibly months because the offender had fired his lawyer.

I was furious—all our planning for nothing. It didn't help that I was already resenting the idea of a trial interfering with our lives as it was.

As I vented, the lawyer for the Crown said very gently, "I've discovered in life that in times like this, I have to act on what I have control of." Those simple words were magic!

No amount of fuming can change something that we have no control of in the first place. Let it go. We need to take back our lives. This is why acceptance and letting go is so key. Acceptance will keep presenting itself as an option.

After we have accepted the situation and disengaged emotionally from the dysfunction of a relationship, we can adjust the boundaries. This is the time of working on the relationship in a respectful, conciliatory effort.

Sometimes we accommodate the problem. We might need to change our expectations in a relationship and make huge allowances for someone's immaturity. For instance, with children or adults who never mature, we need to give them room to make many mistakes.

Sometimes we walk away, dust off our sandals, and carry on.

Whatever way we choose, it's not respectful to just walk away from someone if they don't know what the issues were or why we temporarily disconnected.

In our case, our adjustment was to speak to the care of the murderer with reason and as much compassion as possible. We needed to engage in discussion with the offender and outline the grievance, the impact, and a solution.

Whether we stay in a relationship or leave a relationship, we are bonded with another person because of the experiences we shared. We need to find resolution in love. That is always the last step in the process.

"Love is patient, love is kind. It does not envy, it does not boast, it is not proud. It does not dishonor others, it is not self-seeking, it is not easily angered, it keeps no record of wrongs. Love does not delight in evil but rejoices with the truth. It always protects, always trusts, always hopes, always perseveres."

This sounds like unconditional love, and this is where the other person is concerned. However, the invisible condition is that love is moral. God is moral, and he calls us to be moral. Morality is the application of God's laws regarding our personal private and public behavior.

I can love a criminal bank robber, but I can't drive the getaway car. I can't participate in immoral behavior.

God loves us. God loves justice.

These are two parallel values that might seem contradictory in some circumstances. We as human beings can't really endure the pressure of two equals; we have to choose one or the other, or at least prioritize.

My own formula is to prioritize: put love first, justice second.

The findings of John Gottman, who has been conducting marital-therapy research for twenty-five years, verifies this. His research enables one to predict with a higher degree of accuracy—about 94%—which couples will stay together and which are likely to divorce. The ratio of positive interaction in happy couples is 20 to 1, in conflicted couples is 5 to 1, and in soon-to-divorce couples is .9 to 1.

In other words, if I approach my husband with positive, loving words first and then address my concerns second, we are in a much better situation to stay married—remain in love—and be able to establish a working partnership that might need correction once in a while. In fact, I should make sure that I have about twenty positive interactions for every one correction.

I wonder what this would look like in all of our relationships. What this would look like applied to criminals.

Love in this instance means that we continue to pray for the person who has harmed us. We also continue to fill the vacuum between us with goodness.

Forgiving is heavy work. At first we might not have the emotional muscle to carry it. We will weave all over the place under the load as we adjust to a new reality. Some psychologists have called this emotional uncertainty the "wobble." It's the ability to waver under the weight of life's suffering and trauma without falling down or giving up.

Forgiveness will never be routine and become a habit. Even though we'd prefer everything to go perfectly from beginning to end, anything experimental doesn't work that way. We rarely get it right the first time. Thomas A. Edison, inventor of the light bulb, described experimentation best: "I have not failed. I've just found 10,000 ways that won't work."

Forgiveness is a never-ending process because injustices are never-ending. Not only are there many secondary injustices that result from the first, but the injustices manifest themselves again and again in different forms. After the trial, for example, everything had changed about the case. We had so much more information. In the light of this new information, I had to choose again whether I still wanted to forgive and what that meant in this particular situation.

We have to learn forgiveness again and again. Most of us don't have a photographic memory. We have to learn through repetition, looking at something over and over through different lenses. And in the end, one act of violence may need new forgiveness as each part of us (our minds, heart, bodies, and spirits) processes it in a new way.

This is why, when the Nazarene was asked how often one should forgive, he answered, "I tell you, not seven times, but seventy-seven times"—which essentially meant that you'll never be able to keep track of all the forgiving you have to do.

Chapter 22

THE UNEXPECTED
GROVE OF TREES

I am planting a tree in this bomb crater to
remind us that in the midst of death, there is
life ... and hope.

—ROBERT S. GRAETZ

He was a promising young minister, but he was troubled. "Can I come to see you?" he asked in a hoarse voice.

We met. "I can't forgive my doctor who botched my treatment," he began. "I have a pulpit and a congregation, but I've lost my enthusiasm to preach."

Then he told me his story. As a child, he had been given a promise that he would be a great minister someday, and he had spent all his life pursuing his dream. However, a few years ago the doctor had found a nodule on his vocal cords. Then the surgeon apparently mishandled the surgery. The result was that speaking became difficult. At first he had wondered if his speaking career was over. His speaking career wasn't over, but now it was painful, limited. Frustrated, he was suing the doctor.

We tried to pinpoint where he was stuck.

And then it came out. The real issue wasn't the doctor at all; he was angry with God. He had asked God for healing, and it wasn't happening. "I believe God promised me a beautiful career. I could have pursued something else. I think God tricked me."

I was reminded of a quotation by A. W. Tozer: "We tend by a secret law of the soul to move toward our mental image of God."

I felt for him; I felt life had tricked me as well.

For twenty-six years, I had thought Candace had died lying on her side, abandoned in freezing temperatures. I had been told that freezing was an easy death. One simply fell asleep and never woke up.

As hard as that was for me, it was what I knew and it was therefore what I had to forgive.

Then, during the trial I learned something very different, something I could barely stomach. I learned that a stranger, apparently well-versed in the sexual subculture of bondage, had abducted Candace, hogtied her, strung her up with twine, and suspended her. He had then pleasured himself.

I had to face that—hard as it was. And that was what I had to forgive. We have to name it as our hearts tell us. We can't minimize it, professionalize it. Our hearts need to forgive.

There were bruises on her cheek, knees, legs, and feet. Was she hit by something with a circular head? Was it a hammer? I don't know what happened, but I visualize it from the circumstantial evidence that came out in bits and pieces through the witnesses.

The police said there were indications that he spent some time in the shed. However, at some point, the cold of the plunging temperatures started to seep into the shed. Did he leave her then—escaping into the dark night—leaving her to die that way, hanging, her blood eventually finding its way to the lowest part of her body, as suggested by the evidence of lividity in her legs?

How could a person do that? Who could gain pleasure out of someone writhing in pain?

I felt tricked. For two decades I hadn't known something as important as the fact that my daughter had been tortured.

Knowing about the torture changed something in me. It isn't supposed to make a difference in the forgiveness process, but it did for me. I was suddenly stuck in these questions: What is evil? And where did it come from? Was God part of it? Suddenly, everywhere I went, I was confronted with these questions. Why do bad things happen to good people? What does evil look like? I actually wondered what it would be like to meet evil.

After a presentation in a prison, I met a man on the outskirts of the room, by the door. He seemed so gentle. As we talked, I wondered vaguely why such a nice man was in prison.

He sympathized with me because his children had been murdered too, he told me. I was immediately sympathetic, and I asked about his children. Six children had been murdered, ages two to eleven.

"Six?" My heart broke for him. I quickly jumped to the conclusion that he had then, in sheer rage, done something vengeful that landed him in prison.

I asked about his grief, and we commiserated with each other. I highly respected him for having endured a greater tragedy with the loss of six—I had only one. He had much more to contend with than I did.

But then I asked him if he knew the man who had murdered his children.

I'll never forget the look on his face.

"I did," he said.

I tried to remain calm. "You did—all six of them?"

I remembered their ages—these had not been little babies. How do you kill six children?

He nodded. "It was the hardest thing I had to do.... It wasn't easy. They didn't want to die. I am both the parent of murdered children and also the murderer."

And as I continued to look into his huge eyes filled with pain, he said, "I did it for them. My wife was taking them away from me, and I couldn't let them be ruined."

He then gave me a letter to read that he had written especially for me because he thought, as a writer, a compassionate person, and a parent, I would understand. My compassion failed as I extricated myself from the conversation. But then I read the letter.

Very forcefully, in well-written prose, he gave the explanation for why he had killed his children. His rationale was sane. It was something I could have written if I had followed through with my need to justify avenging the murder of my daughter.

Obviously, evil is not in the face of the person. It isn't in the writing. It is somewhere else very, very deep in their abyss.

I went back to the Bible for a look at the Tree of Good and Evil where it all began. What a shock! When I read the words, "Now the earth was formless and empty, darkness was over the surface of the deep," the words jumped out at me. I immediately recognized it as the perfect description of my abyss. I checked the words of all the translations and read it over and over. I had a sense of the enormity of the chaos, the blackness, the emptiness, and yet the power of a hungry abyss—alive and dead at the same time.

My next questions were, How did that abyss get in me? And where is that abyss now? What did God do with it?

I continued to read the Genesis story in a new head-space. I read how God planted a tree of good and evil in the middle of the garden. There it was: evil, right in the middle of the garden, in the form of a tree.

I'm not sure how I made the leap, but I suddenly saw how plausible it would be for God as the Great Creator to take the evil abyss and wrap up it up with goodness—the only virtue strong enough to hold it—and form a majestic tree. Not as a representation of good and evil as I had been led to believe, but the real thing.

Then God, a moral God who had created moral human beings, warned them not to eat of the tree.

We know what happened next in the story—they were tricked into eating it. Imagine it: Adam and Eve eating something as dark and vile as an abyss—massive, yet condensed. It's a wonder they didn't explode into a million pieces of blackness.

However, even if their bodies survived the eating of it, their souls were damaged. The evil they ingested seemed to act like a spiritual cancer cell manifesting itself in symptoms of what we now call evil or sin. These symptoms of the abyss are extremely important to us, because they are still part of our own DNA.

Adam, being the first person to experience perfection and then evil, is our best authority on what evil means to us as a human race. His first words were, "I heard you in the garden, and I was afraid because I was naked, so I hid." God immediately recognized the change and asked, "Have you eaten from the tree...?" Then Adam displayed another characteristic of the abyss: blame. "The woman you put here with me..." If we follow that line of thinking, it was actually God's fault all along. But was it?

If we go back to the original words, we would translate those words to mean that fear is the first sign of the abyss in us. Adam also had a new sense of falseness, a new sense of pride or egoism, and finally the need to disconnect. These are the sources of evil in us: fear, ego, deceit, a lack of loyalty to each other, no interest in God, and an avoidance of taking responsibility.

Realizing what happened, God moved quickly. He removed them from the garden. He didn't let them near the Tree of Life.

This is the important part. Once the situation was again contained, God gave a short speech about how things would work from now on. In the speech, he hints that he is planning a new order. He is planting this Tree of Forgiveness that grows and grows, and now we can all have access to it in the gardens of our lives.

I don't think it was a particularly good-looking tree at this point in history. I think it must have been a rather strange-looking tree, hardly visible. But it grew and grew and eventually appears again as the tree that the Nazarene died on years later, culminating in the message and power of forgiveness.

What does this mean?

We were tricked—and we will continue to be tricked. But it wasn't God who tricked us. God isn't the only force in the universe. There is a trickster—Adam and Eve fell for the trickster back then, and we do as well.

God could have abandoned his broken project at that point, but the Bible is clear that even though he was tempted to, he couldn't. He loved us too much. Instead, we have this metaphorical Tree of Forgiveness that takes on a new reality when the Nazarene becomes the Messiah.

I became overwhelmed with the responsibility of now trying to live up to our public declaration to forgive. Forgiveness is a complicated concept. The manual—the Bible—is a complicated book. And we are complicated human beings when we are healthy—more so when we are fragmented.

How was I possibly going to know how to navigate this treacherous path in a new traumatized land? What if we failed?

My mind was too traumatized to read a full book on any subject. There wasn't enough time to take a course, yet I knew I was woefully ill-equipped.

I still remember turning over one night, switching on the light, and reaching for my Bible. With a prayer, I opened the book randomly and let my finger slide. It landed miraculously on the perfect verse: "Whether you turn to the right or to the left, your ears will hear a voice behind you, saying, 'This is the way; walk in it.'"

I had a guide! I had access to a voice. I've operated on this principle for the last thirty-two years. I move in whatever direction makes sense or that I feel is God's will, and then I wait for the little voice. Unfortunately, sometimes I don't wait. Sometimes the voice is silent, but often there is a tiny little nudge in the form of written or spoken words or a friend who gives me direction.

This promise of a guide is extremely important in forgiveness. First of all, we feel an emotional reaction— something is wrong. Someone has injured us, and we feel the pain and that first response of anger. Then comes the fork in the road: What are we going to do? Are we going to react quickly and take the main road, or do we take the one less traveled? Forgiveness is always counterintuitive.

At that point there is a rush of loss or a rush of release—sometimes both at the same time. There is a fear of the unknown, the loss of something we hold dear, together with that feeling of shedding a burden and feeling as light as a bird. Soon we feel the responsibility of rebuilding again. We become practical and need to work at filling our loss and fixing what is broken as best we know how.

What we often fail to realize is that this is the perfect time to step out into a new creativity. This is the time to engage in the imagination of the divine and to wonder aloud the possibilities of building something new. Even though God's presence is important throughout, it becomes even more active and integral at the end, the creative end when we need God's imagination to create something new.

In review, I glimpsed this for the first time in the novel *White Banners* when Hannah hears of a kind of forgiveness that *"is the secret renunciation, the giving-up, the letting-go, the sacrifice that nobody understands but the person who does it—that generates inside of you a peculiar power to—"*

"To do what?"

"To do almost anything you like ..."

This promise of power and miracles is also found throughout the Nazarene's teaching. When we move against the norm and reach for the counterintuitive lifestyle of forgiveness, we gain a powerful guide who is capable of doing miracles. The Nazarene promises us the kingdom of heaven, fulfillment, comfort, mercy, an encounter with God, an inheritance, and anything we ask for.

The Tree of Life that we were denied when we were

contaminated becomes available again to us once we partake of forgiveness The fruits of this tree are beautiful: love, joy, peace, forbearance, kindness, goodness, faithfulness, gentleness, and self-control.

Chapter 23

What Is Forgiveness?

We all need to define forgiveness for ourselves. This is my definition.

Because the world is broken—and it is broken in so many ways—forgiveness is a virtue.

We not only forgive, but we also need to be forgiving. It should be part of our character.

Forgiveness is an ancient, overarching, and universal concept.

The concept of forgiveness has been around since the beginning of time. It is hidden in every story that deals with a conflict and the desire for revenge. When we talk about revenge, the alternative is forgiveness. Forgiveness is included in all major religions.

Forgiveness ascribes to a prosocial, optimistic, and counterintuitive mindset.

Forgiveness does not come naturally. It is not the norm. In fact, it is newsworthy. Its foundation is faith, hope, and love ... and the greatest of these is love.

Forgiveness is determined to transform the negative impact of brokenness into goodness in all situations (not just relationships).

The primary purpose of forgiveness is a transformational process that turns evil into good.

Forgiveness is especially visible as a means of mending broken interpersonal relationships through the application of customized, altruistic, moral, innovative, and letting-go processes.

Forgiveness is tested on the complications of our relationships. Forgiveness helps us navigate difficult relationships. Forgiveness can become challenging because each situation is different. It needs to start with unconditional love toward another person.

Forgiveness addresses the moral panic and need for justice in society by fostering truth telling and goodness.

Forgiveness is not about removing ourselves from the world entirely but remaining involved in and contributing to a more peaceful society. It is about word and deed. We not only preach goodness, we also do goodness.

Forgiveness believes that brokenness can be overcome.

Forgiveness is optimistic. It does not give up on this world. It doesn't give up on anyone. If it needs to build a fence around the vulnerable to protect them, it builds walls with gates and doors.

Forgiveness can happen with or without the cooperation of the injurer.

Forgiveness is an autonomous decision. It is not dependent on the response of the other. It is a lifestyle.

If we don't believe that the world is broken, forgiveness makes no sense at all. If we don't believe in the goodness of the creator God, forgiveness makes no sense. Forgiveness is such a huge concept that we may find it difficult to see it all, much like the elephant in the following story:

Once upon a time, there lived six blind men in a village. One day the villagers told them, "Hey, there is an elephant in the village today."

They had no idea what an elephant was. They decided, "Even though we would not be able to see it, let us go and feel it anyway." All of them went where the elephant was. Every one of them touched the elephant.

"Hey, the elephant is a pillar," said the first man, who touched its leg.

"Oh, no! It is like a rope," said the second man, who touched the tail.

"Oh, no! It is like a thick branch of a tree," said the third man, who touched the trunk of the elephant.

"It is like a big hand fan," said the fourth man, who touched the ear of the elephant.

"It is like a huge wall," said the fifth man, who touched the belly of the elephant.

"It is like a solid pipe," said the sixth man, who touched the tusk of the elephant.

They began to argue about the elephant, and every one of them insisted that he was right.

I think this illustrates my experience of forgiveness. Some think it is only a concept, some just a mindset, some think it is only a set of processes between people, some think it is only about redemption, others see it as a means of social action and peacemaking. All those elements are part of it, but forgiveness is strongest when we see the whole. This has been my attempt. But my concept and my experience of forgiveness are still changing and evolving. I'm not sure we will ever know what forgiveness is truly all about till we see from an eternal point of view.

Because we live in a broken world, forgiveness is a virtue that is best described as an ancient, overarching, and universal concept. It ascribes to a prosocial, optimistic, and counterintuitive mindset that is determined to transform the negative impact of the brokenness into goodness in all situations, especially in broken interpersonal relationships. Through the application of customized, altruistic, moral, innovative, and "letting-go" processes, it unpacks the injury in such a way that we can be healed. Forgiveness is also outwardly responsible to address the moral issues and the need for justice in society by fostering truth telling and goodness in justice-making processes. In the end, forgiveness is founded on the belief that brokenness is surmountable—with or without the cooperation of the injurer. No, it is more than surmountable. Each hardship that comes our way can be turned into a blessing with the help of the Creator of this Tree.

WD
March 2, 2016

POSTLUDE: JOSEPH JUSTICE

How does this journey in forgiveness end?

Initially I began this journey of forgiveness for many reasons, but the main reason was simply because I loved the idea of it as an experiment. An experiment is a procedure carried out to support, refute, or validate a hypothesis.

So what has been the result? Has the hypothesis been validated?

After telling my story, I remember one woman looking at me from across the room with a studied measure of impatience. "Well—have you forgiven? Have you forgiven him? Have you met with him?" In other words, have you reconciled?

I hesitated. I have met with him, figuratively. I have met with him almost every day since our daughter was taken. There seems to be a hidden issue in each day that reminds me of my loss and can take me right back to that initial pain in a split second.

But no, I have not met with the man who has been accused of the murder mainly because it is still in process. The trial continues thirty-three years later. There actually hasn't even been an agreed-upon verdict. So until there is a conclusion to this justice process, and even though we sit in the same room, the law prevents us from any interaction. Reconciliation, as such, is not possible.

In fact, there is no resolution of any kind possible in our

case. Often in an injustice, we look for resolution from the offender or at least from some justice process. In our case, we have had no justice or hope of resolution. Imagine if I had waited for it. I would have spent most of my life on the shelf.

So what is the conclusion? What does forgiveness look like for us?

I remember another time when the question was paramount in my mind. I had just been given a speaking assignment to talk about the benefits of forgiveness. Being right in the middle of "letting go," I couldn't think of any. At that point in the process, I was experiencing a lot of emptiness. I was depending on sheer determination—and it was wearing thin. I couldn't deny it. I longed for justice that would end this endless pain.

In desperation I picked up my Bible, randomly opening the pages and letting my finger drift over the page. It landed on the story of Joseph—a young boy sold into slavery who eventually rules not only the country but his brothers who sold him.

At the end of Joseph's life he was able to say to his brothers, "You intended to harm me, but God intended it for good ..."

What kind of justice was this?

There are many justices in this world—traditional justice, restorative justice, real justice, economic, distributive, procedural, retributive, social justice, and probably more— but in the final analysis even though each of these justices are important, they hold little promise of satisfaction for the victim. Most justices are still there to hold the offender accountable with little compensation or even sympathy for the victim.

So if there is no resolution, then what is it?

Actually, we have to change our expectation. It's not about resolution but about overcoming the impact.

Forgiveness is about justices that help us overcome.

There is the Joseph justice. Joseph distinguished himself in everything he did. He was never mired in anger and self-pity but worked hard and remained moral and loyal. These choices promoted him—let him rise to the top—and positioned him as a ruler so that eventually he even ruled over his brothers.

This isn't uncommon in the forgiveness process. The forgiving victims at times find themselves in control of the destiny of the offender. I call this the Joseph justice.

Another outcome could be called poetic justice. This is when goodness is ultimately rewarded mysteriously, and vice is punished more out of the natural causation of human nature than our traditional-justice processes.

We say, "One reaps what one sows" or "What goes around comes around."

There is also a kind of transformational justice. This is when the initial evil act is deliberately cocooned in goodness. The injustice is put on hold and kept in place while we continue to cover it with good acts and a positive learning attitude. The miracle is that when we look back, it has been transformed into something beautiful, like a butterfly. And we find that we treasure the goodness—the learning or the skill or whatever emerges—and are actually thankful for it.

Again like Joseph we can see that it was intended for evil, but God transforms it into good.

We have found these forms of justices are often more satisfying than the traditional-justice efforts.

Recently, at the end of a long and tiring but wonderful day, I looked across the bed at Cliff, grateful for the day we had spent together enjoying our fun-loving, inspiring children and their little ones.

"I am really happy," I said.

He looked at me. "I am too."

We stared at each other. "Really happy," we said again.

How did we get here?

There was no logical rationale for our happiness.

And that's what forgiveness does. Forgiveness, I believe, leads to this kind of Joseph, poetic, and transformational justice that truly satisfies us. If we only stick to it and persist along this route, we will end with a pervasive sense of win-win.

Surprised by our happiness, we said, "Let's not tell anyone." We actually felt guilty for being so happy. It felt as if we were betraying Candace—as if we were somehow being irresponsible.

But then we caught ourselves again. Justice was happening. Candace was thriving. Even though Candace had been murdered, she was still alive. Her memory and legacy were more powerful than any of ours. And the man accused of murdering our child had not fared as well. Sometimes we have to wait until the end of the story to see the scales of justice tip in our favor.

There was one more thing. Having scraped the bottom of life as we had, there is simply nothing more divine than to resurface into the sunshine and feel that warmth, that healing, and that beauty. On top of the feeling of fullness, there is that extra sense of victory. We have seen the worst; fear was gone. It felt as if nothing could faze us now. We were so thankful for everything—even the experience of surviving a tragedy.

Gratitude brings even more happiness, as happiness brings gratitude. It is a wonderful cycle—a vortex for good rather than the abyss.

We initially want a justice that will end with a one and one equals two. We want a justice to be a logical accounting that matches the loss. But with forgiveness we have the privilege of a new justice … a God-driven justice in which one and one equals three, if not four.

So even though we haven't had the logical-accounting justice, we no longer require it because the more poetic justice of forgiveness is so much more satisfying.

So, like Joseph I can truly say, "You might have meant it for evil, but God meant it for good."

Now, I am just grateful that long ago—actually decades ago—I experimented with that metaphorical forgiveness tree that was there for us, that was prepared for us right in the beginning of time.

I am grateful for that ancient tree—planted so long ago—that continues to set our spirits free.

FOR FURTHER READING ON FORGIVENESS

Affinito, Mona Gustafson. *When to Forgive: A Healing Guide to Help You.* Oakland, CA: New Harbinger Publications, 1999.

Allender, Dan B., and Tremper Longman III. *Bold Love.* Colorado Springs, CO: NavPress, 1992.

Augsburger, David. *Caring Enough to Forgive: True Forgiveness.* Ventura, CA: Regal, 1981.

Baumeister, Roy F. *Evil: Inside Human Violence and Cruelty.* New York: Holt Paperbacks, 1999.

Beattie, Melody. *Codependent No More: How to Stop Controlling Others and Start Caring for Yourself.* Center City, MN: Hazelden, 1992.

Borris-Dunchunstang, Eileen R. *Finding Forgiveness: A 7-Step Program for Letting Go of Anger and Bitterness.* New York: McGraw Hill, 2010.

Bradshaw, John. *Healing the Shame That Binds You.* Deerfield Beach, FL: Health Communications, 2005.

Brown, Brené. *Daring Greatly: How the Courage to Be Vulnerable Transforms the Way We Live, Love, Parent, and Lead.* New York: Avery, 2012.

Cantacuzino, Marina. *The Forgiveness Project: Stories for a Vengeful Age.* London: Jessica Kingsley, 2015.

Carruthers, Avril. *Freedom from Toxic Relationships: Moving On from the Family, Work, and Relationship Issues That Bring You Down.* New York: Penguin, 2013.

Carter, Les. *The Anger Trap: Free Yourself from the Frustrations That Sabotage Your Life.* San Francisco: Jossey Bass, 2004.

Cloud, Henry. *Changes That Heal: The Four Shifts That Make Everything Better and That Anyone Can Do*. Grand Rapids: Zondervan, 1993.

———. *Necessary Endings: The Employees, Businesses, and Relationships That All of Us Have to Give Up in Order to Move Forward*. New York: HarperBusiness, 2011.

Cloud, Henry, and John Townsend. *Boundaries: When to Say Yes, When to Say No to Take Control of Your Life*. Grand Rapids: Zondervan, 1992.

———. *God Will Make a Way: What to Do When You Don't Know What to Do*. Nashville: Thomas Nelson, 2006.

———. *How to Have That Difficult Conversation*. Grand Rapids: Zondervan, 2015.

Covey, Stephen R. *The 8th Habit: From Effectiveness to Greatness*. New York: Free Press, 2005.

Dostoevsky, Fyodor. *Crime and Punishment*. New York: Dover, 2001.

Douglas, Lloyd C. *White Banners*. New York: Pocket Books, 1946.

Dunwoody, Gregory. *Compassion and Forgiveness: Inheriting the Wisdom of Our Spiritual Traditions*. Winnipeg: Echo Spiritual Publications, 2000.

Enright, Robert D., and Joanna North. *Exploring Forgiveness*. Madison: University of Wisconsin Press, 1998.

Enright, Robert D. *The Forgiving Life: A Pathway to Overcoming Resentment and Creating a Legacy of Love*. Washington, DC: American Psychological Association, 2012.

Frankl, Victor E. *Man's Search for Meaning*. New York: Pocket Books, 1997.

Gladwell, Malcolm. *David and Goliath: Underdogs, Misfits, and the Art of Battling Giants*. New York: Little, Brown and Company, 2013.

————. *Outliers: The Story of Success.* New York: Little, Brown and Company, 2008.

Goll, Jim W. *Father Forgive Us! Finding Freedom from the Sins of the Past.* Shippensburg, PA: Destiny Image, 2000.

Greaves, Stuart. *False Justice: Unveiling the Truth about Social Justice.* Shippensburg, PA: Destiny Image, 2012.

Griswold, Charles L. *Forgiveness: A Philosophical Exploration.* New York: Cambridge University Press, 2007.

Griswold, Charles L., and David Konstan. *Ancient Forgiveness.* New York: Cambridge University Press, 2007.

Hemfelt, Robert, Frank Minirth, and Paul Meier. *Love Is a Choice: The Definitive Book on Letting Go of Unhealthy Relationships.* Nashville: Nelson, 2003.

Herman, Judith Lewis. *Trauma and Recovery: The Aftermath of Violence—From Domestic Abuse to Political Terror.* New York: Basic Books, 2015.

Hybels, Bill. *Just Walk across the Room: Simple Steps Pointing People to Faith.* Grand Rapids: Zondervan, 2006.

Jakes, T. D. *Let It Go: Forgive So You Can Be Forgiven.* New York: Atria Books, 2013.

Janoff-Bulman, Ronnie. *Shattered Assumptions: Towards a New Psychology of Trauma.* New York: Free Press, 2002.

Jones, L. Gregory. *Embodying Forgiveness: A Theological Analysis.* Grand Rapids: Eerdmans, 1995.

Kendall, R. T. *Total Forgiveness: When Everything in You Wants to Hold a Grudge, Point a Finger, and Remember the Pain, God Wants You to Lay It All Aside.* Lake Mary, FL: Charisma House, 2007.

Klug, Lyn. *A Forgiving Heart: Prayers for Blessing and Reconciliation.* Minneapolis: Augsburg Fortress, 2003.

Kushner, Harold S. *When Bad Things Happen to Good People.* New York: Anchor Books, 2004.

Ladner, Lorne. *The Lost Art of Compassion: Discovering the Practice of Happiness in the Meeting of Buddhism and Psychology.* San Francisco: HarperOne, 2004.

LaHaye, Tim. *How to Win over Depression.* Grand Rapids: Zondervan, 1996.

Larsen, Earnie. *From Anger to Forgiveness: A Practical Guide to Breaking the Negative Power of Anger and Achieving Reconciliation.* New York: Ballantine, 1992.

Lewis, C. S. *Miracles.* San Francisco: HarperOne, 2015.

Luskin, Fred. *Forgive for Good: A PROVEN Prescription for Health and Happiness.* San Fransico: HarperOne, 2003.

Martin, David G. *Counseling and Therapy Skills.* Long Grove, IL: Waveland, 2011.

May, Rollo. *Love and Will.* New York: W. W. Norton, 2007.

McCullough, Michael E., Kenneth I. Pargament, and Carl E.Thoresen. *Forgiveness: Theory, Research, and Practice.* New York: Guilford, 2001.

McVey, Steve. *A Divine Invitation: Experiencing the Romance of God's Amazing Love.* Eugene, OR: Harvest House, 2002.

Miller, Beth. *The Woman's Book of Resilience: 12 Qualities to Cultivate.* Newburyport, MA: Conari, 2005.

Moroney, Shannon. *Through the Glass.* New York: Gallery Books, 2014.

Nakazawa, Donna Jackson. *Childhood Disrupted: How Your Biography Becomes Your Biology, and How You Can Heal.* New York: Atria Books, 2015.

Nathanson, Donald L. *Shame and Pride: Affect, Sex, and the Birth of Self.* New York: W. W. Norton, 2015.

Nouwen, Henri J. M. *Home Tonight: Further Reflections on the Parable of the Prodigal Son.* New York: Image, 2009.

Peck, M. Scott. *People of the Lie: The Hope for Healing Human Evil.* New York: Touchstone Books, 1998.

Plett, Jake. *Valley of Shadows.* Beaverlodge, AB: Horizon House, 1976.

Reivich, Karen, and Andrew Shatte. *The Resilience Factor: 7 Keys to Finding Your Inner Strength and Overcoming Life's Hurdles.* New York: Broadway Books, 2003.

Rohr, Richard. *Falling Upward: A Spirituality for the Two Halves of Life.* San Francisco: Jossey-Bass, 2011.

Rupp, Joyce. *May I Have This Dance? An Invitation to Faithful Prayer throughout the Year.* Notre Dame, IN: Ave Maria, 2007.

Simon, Sidney, and Suzanne Simon. *Forgiveness: How to Make Peace with Your Past and Get on with Your Life.* New York: Grand Central, 1991.

Smedes, Lewis B. *The Art of Forgiving: When You Need to Forgive and Don't Know How.* New York: Ballantine, 1997.

———. *Forgive and Forget: Healing the Hurts We Don't Deserve.* San Francisco: HarperOne, 2007.

Stone, Douglas, Bruce Patton, and Sheila Heen. *Difficult Conversations: How to Discuss What Matters Most.* New York: Penguin, 2010.

Tillich, Paul. *Love, Power, and Justice: Ontological Analysis and Ethical Application.* New York: Oxford University Press, 1960.

Tolle, Eckhart. *A New Earth: Awakening to Your Life's Purpose.* New York: Penguin, 2008.

Weems, Ann. *Psalms of Lament.* Louisville: Westminster John Knox, 1995.

Wolfelt, Alan D. *The Journey through Grief: Reflections on Healing.* Fort Collins, CO: Companion, 2003.

Wolin, Steven J., and Sybil Wolin. *The Resilient Self: How Survivors of Troubled Families Rise above Adversity.* New York: Villard, 1993.

Woolford, Andrew. *The Politics of Restorative Justice: A Critical Introduction.* Winnipeg: Fernwood, 2010.

Worthington, Everett L. Jr. *Forgiving and Reconciling: Bridges to Wholeness and Hope.* Downers Grove, IL: InterVarsity Press, 2003.

————. *A Just Forgiveness: Responsible Healing without Excusing Injustice.* Downers Grove, IL: InterVarsity Press, 2009.

Yancey, Phillip. *Vanishing Grace: Whatever Happened to the Good News?* Grand Rapids: Zondervan, 2014.

————. *What's So Amazing about Grace?* Grand Rapids: Zondervan, 2002.

Young, William P. *The Shack: Where Tragedy Confronts Eternity.* Los Angeles: Windblown Media, 2007.

NOTES

CHAPTER 1: THE ENDING AND THE BEGINNING

17 *now a parent of a murdered child.* I didn't know it at the time, but this first encounter with another parent of a murdered child was also my introduction to the *aftermath of murder persona.* He was manifesting trauma issues that are distinct to people who had experienced violence. I later wrote about this in a book entitled *Confronting the Horror: The Aftermath of Violence* (Winnipeg: Amity, 2002), 8.

17 *My identity was at stake.* Here I encountered *identity devastation.* Our identity changes after encountering violence (ibid., 85).

18 *Everyone was a potential murderer.* Here I encountered a new kind of fear—*terror trauma.* Our feelings of safety are destroyed when we experience violence or the threat of violence (ibid., 35).

20 *began to tell his story.* Here I encountered *story fragmentation.* The first reaction to something as traumatic as murder is disconnection and numbness. Many victims describe a state of fluid emotion with no words. For some this is followed by a compulsion to tell the story over and over again to whoever will listen (ibid., 21).

20 *There were no tears as he talked.* Here I encountered *grief displacement.* After a murder act, the mourning process can be deliberately repressed until the trial has taken place. Since some issues of murder are never resolved, it is not uncommon for grief to be permanently lost in the aftermath of murder (ibid., 51).

20 *he had told his story many times.* Here I encountered *time/ memory warp.* Many victims describe murder trauma as a

time of being unable to control their minds. It becomes a torturous replay that can't be stopped (ibid., 65).

20 *smoldering with an inner rage*. Here I encountered *uncontrollable rage*. This murder trauma is an irrational emotion that can begin to control the victim (ibid., 143).

21 *meticulously and in detail*. Here I encountered *truth dilemma*. After murder, crime victims have an obsessive need to know exactly what happened and why (ibid., 131).

21 *ranted against the justice system*. Here I encountered *justice revictimization*. Most crime victims are appalled to discover that they are not even represented in the courtroom as individuals. They have absolutely no position or voice concerning the proceedings (ibid., 177).

21 *knew every detail of this offender's public and private life*. Here I encountered what I have called the *victim/offender trauma bond*. It is important to note that not only are the victims bonded with the offenders; often everyone who was primarily in the experience remain bonded somehow—like an alumni of the bond (ibid., 163).

21 *angry with the media*. Here I encountered what I call *blame/ guilt confusion*. We often choose our target of blame based not on reason or evidence but on safety and vindication. We tend to scapegoat (ibid., 119).

21 *lost so much—everything*. Here I encountered what I call *disabling harm*. As a result of the initial harm caused by murder or any other crime, there are series of less obvious spiraling losses that we will continue to experience (ibid., 105).

21 *just wanted it to be over*. Here I encountered what I call *unsatisfactory closure*. We yearn to find closure and to find a way of moving on, but because the overall impact of violence is so astronomical, the aftermath can never be contained (ibid., 203).

23 *cold winter night alone and despondent*. Here I encountered

what I call *paralyzing despair*. Not being able to move beyond the aftermath of murder, we become stuck. This is the accumulative result of all the other issues. We lose hope of ever being able to recover (ibid., 229).

23 *There had to be another way.* Here I encountered what I call *recovery controversy.* There is no agreed upon process to recover from the murder of a child. There is only a continual pressure to conform to one process or another (ibid., 215).

CHAPTER 2: THE ONLY QUESTION

26 *My abyss would not be denied.* I wrote two novels about my experience as an invisible child: *Path of the Heart,* Ava Series 1 (Winnipeg: Amity, 2012) and *Echo of the Soul,* Ava Series 2 (Winnipeg: Amity, 2012).

27 *The term forgive.* Paul M. Hughes, "Forgiveness," *Stanford Encyclopedia of Philosophy*, December 23, 2014, http://plato .stanford.edu/entries/forgiveness/.

CHAPTER 3: THE EMOTIONAL LANDMINES

38 *separate us into four parts.* The temperaments had their origins in the Four Humors—choleric, melancholy, sanguine, and phlegmatic—introduced by Hippocrates. Beginning with Homer in 750 BC, Plato, Tolstoy, Jung, and Myers & Briggs have always broken humans down to four basic personality types. David Keirsey, *Please Understand Me II: Temperament, Character, Intelligence* (Del Mar, CA: Promethesus Nemesis, 1998).

38 *mind, heart, body, and spirit.* According to Dr. Rose Roberts of the Public Health Agency of Canada, "The most common health model found in the literature and the oral tradition of Aboriginal peoples is the medicine wheel model. Actual medicine wheels are circular stone formations found in all

parts of North America. The term *medicine wheel* has been borrowed from these stone structures and applied to the theory of health and other areas of Aboriginal traditions. The medicine wheel is a circle, which means there is no end and no beginning. The same could be said for one's health status. The four areas of the wheel are intellectual, emotional, spiritual, and physical. Some Aboriginal people believe that all four areas have to be in balance if one is to be in an optimum state of health; in other words, if any of the four areas are out of balance, then the individual becomes ill" (Rose Roberts, "Appendix G: Working with Aboriginal Individuals," Public Health Agency of Canada, http://www .phac-aspc.gc.ca/sfv-avf/sources/nfnts/nfnts-sensi/appendix -annexe-g-eng.php).

39 *forgiving as a complete person.* In Matthew 22:37, Jesus repeats this: "Love the Lord your God with all your heart and with all your soul and with all your mind"; Mark 12:30: "Love the Lord your God with all your heart and with all your soul and with all your mind and with all your strength"; Luke 10:27: "He answered, 'Love the Lord your God with all your heart and with all your soul and with all your strength and with all your mind'; and, 'Love your neighbor as yourself.'"

CHAPTER 4: THE WAY

48 *Douglas.* Lloyd C. Douglas, *White Banners* (New York: Houghton Mifflin, 1936).

49 *"To do almost anything you like"*: Ibid., 262.

50 *"greatest of these is love"*: 1 Corinthians 13:13.

51 *Even chimpanzees can forgive.* "And just as with revenge, research has found that forgiveness is also widespread across the animal kingdom, offering further evidence of its evolutionary significance. More than two decades ago,

primatologist Frans de Waal and a colleague published results showing that friendly behaviors such as kissing, submissive vocal sounds, touching, and embracing were actually quite common after chimpanzees' aggressive conflicts. In fact, these were the chimpanzees' typical responses to aggressive conflicts. The researchers observed 350 aggressive encounters and found that only 50, or 14 percent, of those encounters were preceded by some sort of friendly contact. However, 179, or 51 percent, of the aggressive encounters were followed by friendly contact. This was a staggering discovery.... Chimps kiss and make up in the same way people do" (Michael E. McCullough, "The Forgiveness Instinct," Greater Good in Action, March 1, 2008, https://www.google.ca/webhp?sourceid=chrome -instant&ion=1&espv=2&ie=UTF-8#q=the%20 forgiveness%20instinct. This essay is excerpted from the author's *Beyond Revenge: The Evolution of the Forgiveness Instinct* [San Francisco: John Wiley & Sons, 2008]).

51 *Even a child can understand forgiveness.* "A new study answers affirmatively, finding that children develop a sense of fairness before they are two years of age. University of Illinois researchers said that they found that 19- and 21-month-old infants have a general expectation of fairness, and they can apply it appropriately to different situations" (Rick Nauert, *"Infants Understand Concept of Fairness,"* PsychCentral, http:// psychcentral.com/news/2012/02/20/infants-understand -concept-of-fairness/35049.html).

51 *"assurance about what we do not see"*: Hebrews 11:1.

Chapter 5: Letting Go of the Happy Ending

57 *"glorify your Father in heaven"*: Matthew 5:14–16.

57 *the word "good" is* kalos. Why would Jesus ask us to parade our

good deeds when in Matthew 6:1 he warns us to be careful not to practice our righteousness in front of others? And how was I, a broken victim, to shine good deeds? However, when one looks back into the Greek of the word translated as "good," kalos, we find that it means lovely, beautiful, helpful, honest, useful, or well adapted to its purpose or end. Originally, it referred to beauty of form. Of all the words, I noticed that it also means honesty. It could mean shining forth a beautiful integrity before everyone. For me, this is doable. We might not have the exemplary life of service that Mother Theresa has, but we can all have that wonderful integrity that comes from knowing our weaknesses and seeking truth.

CHAPTER 6: LETTING GO OF FEAR

63 *Albrecht.* Karl Albrecht, "*The (Only) Five Fears We All Share: When We Know Where They Really Come From, We Can Start to Control Them,*" *Psychology Today*, March 22, 2012, https://www.psychologytoday.com/blog/brainsnacks/201203/the-only-5-fears-we-all-share.

64 *Margee Kerr.* Edith Zimmerman, "The Science of Fear: An Interview with 'Scare Expert' Margee Kerr," *The Hairpin*, September 19, 2012, https://thehairpin.com/the-science-of-fear-an-interview-with-scare-expert-margee-kerr-efb081066a71#.2v390jq53.

65 *"kingdom of heaven"*: Matthew 5:3.

65 *fearful, cowering disposition.* The Greek word here for "poor" (*ptōchos*) is related to the Greek verb *ptēssō*, meaning "to crouch, cower."

CHAPTER 7: LETTING GO OF MY GRIEF

69 *"fertile soil of you"*: lyrics from Michael W. Smith, "Friends," *Change Your World* (Reunion Records, 1992).

70 *"Lord of them"*: Ibid.

71 *Michael W. Smith*. Concert took place on March 3, 1985.

73 *"they will be comforted"*: Matthew 5:4.

74 *Worden*. William J. Worden, *Grief Counseling and Grief Therapy: A Handbook for the Mental Health Practitioner*, 4th ed. (New York: Springer, 2009), 39.

CHAPTER 8: LETTING GO OF MY EGO

82 *"You have heard that it was said"*: From the Sermon on the Mount: Matthew 5:38–42, 45.

CHAPTER 9: LETTING GO OF MY NARROW FAITH

91 *"delivereth them"*: King James Version.

CHAPTER 10: LETTING GO OF THE OLD ME

95 *Gazzaniga*. As quoted by Adam Waytz, "The Psychology of Social Status," *Scientific American*, December 8, 2009, http://www.scientificamerican.com/article/the-psychology-of-social/.

95 *Schlosser*. Eric Schlosser, "A Grief like No Other," *Atlantic Monthly* 280.3 (1997): 2.

96 *Redmond*. Lula M. Redmond, "Sudden Violent Death," in *Living with Grief: After Sudden Loss Suicide, Homicide, Accident, Heart Attack, Stroke*, ed. Kenneth J. Doka (New York: Routledge, 1996), 62.

CHAPTER 12: LETTING GO OF MY GUILT AND BLAME

110 *Jordan.* Tom Jordan, "Are You Being Blamed?," *Love-Life Learning Centre*, http://lovelifelearningcenter.com .previewdns.com/are-you-being-blamed/.

111 *"measured to you"*: Matthew 7:1–2.

111 *the word "judge."* The word translated here as "judge" is from krinō, which means "to decide, separate, think, come to a choice." It "typically refers to making a determination of right or wrong.... We can only *judge* (2919 /krinō) accurately by *intelligent comparison and contrast* based on God's word, i.e. to approve (prefer) what is correct and reject what is inferior (wrong)" (James Strong, "2919. krinō," *Strong's Concordance*, Bible Hub, http://biblehub.com/str/greek/2919.htm).

CHAPTER 13: LETTING GO OF MY NEED TO KNOW

117 *"Each day has enough trouble"*: Matthew 6:25, 34.

117 *outside our control.* Dennis Marquandt states that the word used by Matthew (translated here as "worry") is the Greek term merimnaō. "It is a combination of two smaller words, merizō, meaning 'to divide,' and nous, meaning 'mind.' In other words, a person who is anxious suffers from a divided mind, leaving him or her disquieted and distracted. Worry occurs when we assume responsibility for things that are outside our control. And I love the Lord's solution: 'Only a few things are necessary, really only one'" (see Luke 10:42 NIV; Dennis Marquandt, "The Worry Rule," Northern New England District Assemblies of God, http://www.nnedaog .org/sermons/SERRULE2.HTM).

CHAPTER 14: LETTING GO OF MY RAGE

125 *"Anger can serve"*: Neel Burton, "Why Anger Is Pointless," *Psychology Today*, August 20, 2012,

https://www.psychologytoday.com/blog/hide-and
-seek/201208/why-anger-is-pointless.

125 *ten to fourteen times a day.* Stephen Gislason, *I and Thou*
(Sechelt, BC: Persona, 2015), 89.

126 *"subject to judgment"*: Matthew 5:21–22. There are two
different Hebrew words (ratsakh; mut) and two Greek
words (phoneuō; apokteinō) for "to murder" and "to kill."
One means "to murder" while the other means "to put to
death." The former is that which is prohibited by the Ten
Commandments.

126 *Smedes.* Lewis Smedes, *Forgive and Forget: Healing the Hurts We
Don't Deserve* (New York: Harper & Row, 1984), 25.

CHAPTER 15: LETTING GO OF MY
OBSESSION WITH THE OFFENDER

131 *Project Angel.* "Project Angel Leads to Arrest in 1984
Candace Derksen Homicide," Winnipeg Police Service,
May 16, 2007, http://www.winnipeg.ca/police/
press/2007/05may/2007_05_16.stm.

132 *she pledged forgiveness.* Julie Horbal, "Mother Hasn't Really
Forgiven," *WinnipegFIRST*, May 16, 2007, http://www
.winnipegfirst.ca/article/2007/05/16/mother_hasnt_really
_forgiven.

132 *Winnipeg Free Press article.* Bruce Owen, "Girl's Parents
Unsure about Forgiving Killer: 'But It Is Something We
Strive For,'" *Winnipeg Free Press*, May 17, 2007, p. A3.

132 *"love your enemies"*: Matthew 5:44.

134 *Smedes.* Lewis B. Smedes, *The Art of Forgiving: When You Need
to Forgive and Don't Know How* (New York: Random House,
1996), 159.

135 *"in all cultures, in all times"*: Ibid., 151.

135 *"love your enemies"*: Matthew 5:43–45.

CHAPTER 16: LETTING GO OF MY JUSTICE FANTASY

142 *Smedes.* Smedes, *Forgive and Forget*, 6.

143 *"Blessed are the peacemakers"*: Matthew 5:9.

143 *Pounds.* Wil Pounds, "Matthew 5:9: Peacemakers," *Abide in Christ*, 2006, http://www.abideinchrist.com/messages/mat5v9.html.

144 *"paid the last penny"*: Matthew 5:25–26.

146 *A reporter wrote.* James Turner, "Crown Turning to High Court in Derksen Case," *Winnipeg Free Press*, November 26, 2013, p. A6.

CHAPTER 17: LETTING GO OF EASY RESOLUTION

149 *reputation, career, or family members.* Gadadhara Pandit Dasa, "Revenge or Forgiveness: Which Road Do You Walk?," *Huffington Post*, April 01, 2014, http://www.huffingtonpost.com/gadadhara-pandit-dasa/revenge-or-forgiveness-wh_b_5063444.html.

151 *"Blessed are the merciful"*: Matthew 5:7.

152 *not many know how to forgive.* "In a large representative sampling of American people on various religious topics in 1988, the Gallup Organization found that 94% said it was important to forgive, but 85% said they needed some outside help to be able to forgive. However, not even regular prayer was found to be effective" (https://en.wikipedia.org/wiki/Forgiveness).

152 *Washington, DC.* To the Theological Forum on Crime Victims and the Church, a theological and practical exploration of victimization, justice, evil and forgiveness, organized by Neighbors Who Care and Prison Fellowship Ministries, October 10–11, 1997.

153 *hand-picked theologians.* Presenters at the October 10–11, 1997 Washington Forum were Dr. Carl F. H. Henry, Dr. Elizabeth

Achtemeier, Dr. Harold Dean Trulear, Charles W. Colson, Dr
Miroslav Volf, Dr. Dan Allender, Dr. Nicholas Wolterstorff, Dr.
Howard Zehr, Dr. L. Gregory Jones, and Mary White.

153 *published in a book.* Lisa Barnes Lampman and Michelle D.
Shattuck, eds., *God and the Victim: Theological Reflections on
Evil, Victimization, Justice, and Forgiveness* (Grand Rapids:
Eerdmans; Washington, DC: Neighbors Who Care, 1999).

CHAPTER 18: LETTING GO OF MY SELF-PITY

161 *Frankl.* Viktor E. Frankl, *Man's Search for Meaning* (New York:
Simon & Shuster, 1984), 86.

CHAPTER 19: LETTING GO OF CLOSURE

168 *"Blessed are those who hunger"*: Matthew 5:6.
170 *The news report stated.* Mike McIntyre, "Guilty Verdict Ends
26-Year Saga," *Winnipeg Free Press*, February 19, 2011, p. A5.

CHAPTER 20: THE NEVER-ENDING
PROCESS, STAGE ONE

176 *Widrich.* Leo Widrich, "The Science of Storytelling: Why
Telling a Story is the Most Powerful Way to Activate Our
Brains," *Lifehacker*, December 05, 2012, http://lifehacker
.com/5965703/the-science-of-storytelling-why-telling-a
-story-is-the-most-powerful-way-to-activate-our-brains.

177 *Hall.* Edward Hall, *Beyond Culture* (New York: Anchor, 2007),
207.

177 *Senge.* Peter M. Senge, *The Fifth Discipline: The Art & Practice
of the Learning Organization*, rev. ed. (New York: Doubleday,
2006), 14–15.

178 *overcome it with good.* Romans 12:21: "Do not be overcome by
evil, but overcome evil with good."

180 *"seventy-seven times"*: Matthew 18:21–22.

CHAPTER 21: THE NEVER-ENDING PROCESS, STAGE TWO

187 *"Do you love me?"* The story can be found in John 21:15–19.

189 *Merton.* As quoted in Matthew Fox, "A Spirituality Called Compassion," *Religious Education* 73.3 (1978): 292.

190 *"Get behind me, Satan."* Matthew 16:23: "Jesus turned and said to Peter, 'Get behind me, Satan! You are a stumbling block to me; you do not have in mind the concerns of God, but merely human concerns.'"

193 *"Love is patient"*: 1 Corinthians 13:4–7.

193 *God loves us.* John 3:16: "For God so loved the world that he gave his one and only Son, that whoever believes in him shall not perish but have eternal life."

193 *God loves justice.* Isaiah 61:8: "For I, the LORD, love justice."

193 *Gottman.* John Mordechai Gottman and Sybil Carrère, "Predicting Divorce among Newlyweds from the First Three Minutes of a Marital Conflict Discussion," *Family Process* 38.3 (1999), 293–301.

194 *"wobble."* Donna Jackson Nakazawa, *Childhood Disrupted: How Your Biography Becomes Your Biology, and How You Can Heal* (New York: Atria Books, 2015), 60.

194 *Edison.* As quoted in Erica P. Hendry, "7 Epic Fails," Smithsonian.com, November 20, 2013, http://www .smithsonianmag.com/innovation/7-epic-fails-brought -to-you-by-the-genius-mind-of-thomas-edison -180947786/?no-ist.

CHAPTER 22: THE UNEXPECTED GROVE OF TREES

197 *Tozer.* A. W. Tozer, *The Knowledge of the Holy* (Glendale, CA: Bibliotech Press, 2016), 1.

200 *"Now the earth was formless"*: Genesis 1:2.

201 *"I heard you in the garden"*: Genesis 3:10.

201 *"Have you eaten from the tree"*: Genesis 3:11.

201 *"The woman you put here with me"*: Genesis 3:12.

203 *"This is the way; walk in it"*: Isaiah 30:21.

204 *White Banners.* Lloyd C. Douglas, *White Banners* (New York: Pocket Books, 1946), 262.

205 *The fruits of this tree.* See Galatians 5:22–23.

CHAPTER 23: WHAT IS FORGIVENESS?

206 *Because the world is broken.* "When evolutionary biologists Martin Daly and Margo Wilson looked at data on 60 different societies from around the world, they tried to determine how many of those societies showed evidence of blood feuds, capital punishment, or the desire for blood revenge. They found that 57 of the 60 societies they examined—95 percent—had 'some reference to blood feud or capital punishment as an institutionalized practice, or specific accounts of particular cases or, at the least, some articulate expression of the desire for blood revenge.'

'What our survey suggests,' Daly and Wilson write in their book *Homicide*, 'is that the inclination to blood revenge is experienced by people in all cultures, and that the act is therefore unlikely to be altogether "absent" anywhere'" (Michael E. McCullough, "The Forgiveness Instinct," March 1, 2008, Greater Good in Action, http://greatergood .berkeley.edu/article/item/forgiveness_instinct).

206 *so many ways—forgiveness.* This definition is inspired by Aristotle, who defined *virtue* as having certain characteristics, such as "the shaping (habituating) of a passion or emotion or disposition (moral education in short); being concerned with both feelings and actions; requiring a central role of practical reason or judgment; and assuming a conception of the good which the agent aims in molding his or her character"

(Charles L. Griswold, *Forgiveness: A Philosophical Exploration* [New York: Cambridge University Press, 2007], 17).

206 *is a virtue.* "I believe that all these claims are true of forgiveness. More precisely, the admirable trait of being disposed to forgiveness (in the right way, on the occasion, and such, as determined by practical reasons)—the quality predicated of a forgiving person's character—is 'forgivingness' on analogy, say, with 'courageousness.' Forgiveness is the moral state of affairs that follows upon the expression of the settled character trait in question, and is either completed or underway (forgiveness can carry a 'present participle' sense). Forgiveness is what the forgiveness expresses, it is what a forgiving person's virtue of forgiveness gives rise to (under the specified conditions, and so on). Following standard practice, however, I will be speaking of the virtue of forgiveness, just as one normally would when, say, defining the virtue of courage" (Griswold, *Forgiveness*, 17).

206 *ancient.* Forgiveness has been encouraged for thousands of years by major world religions. Adherents have claimed that forgiveness yields numerous emotional and spiritual benefits and can dramatically transform one's life. Mark S. Rye et al., "Religious Perspectives on Forgiveness," in *Forgiveness: Theory, Research, and Practice*, ed. Michael E. McCullough, Kenneth I. Pargament, and Carl E. Thoresen (New York: Guilford, 2000), 17.

208 *the elephant.* "The Elephant and the Blind Man," Jainworld .com, http://www.jainworld.com/literature/story25.htm.

POSTLUDE: JOSEPH JUSTICE

211 *"God intended it for good"*: Genesis 50:20.